FUCKING
GOOD
MANNERS

FUCKING GOOD MANNERS

SIMON GRIFFIN

ICON

Published in the UK in 2019 by Icon Books Ltd, Omnibus Business
Centre, 39–41 North Road, London N7 9DP
email: info@iconbooks.com • www.iconbooks.com

Sold in the UK, Europe and Asia by Faber & Faber Ltd,
Bloomsbury House, 74–77 Great Russell Street, London
WC1B 3DA or their agents

Distributed in the UK, Europe and Asia by Grantham Book
Services, Trent Road, Grantham NG31 7XQ

Distributed in Australia and New Zealand by Allen & Unwin
Pty Ltd, PO Box 8500, 83 Alexander Street, Crows Nest, NSW 2065

Distributed in South Africa by Jonathan Ball, Office B4,
The District, 41 Sir Lowry Road, Woodstock 7925

Distributed in India by Penguin Books India, 7th Floor, Infinity
Tower – C, DLF Cyber City, Gurgaon 122002, Haryana

Distributed in the USA by Publishers Group West, 1700 Fourth
Street, Berkeley, CA 94710

Distributed in Canada by Publishers Group Canada, 76 Stafford
Street, Unit 300, Toronto, Ontario M6J 2S1

ISBN: 978-178578-551-1

Typeset in Cochin by Marie Doherty

Printed and bound in Great Britain by Clays Ltd, Elcograf S.p.A

For Mum and Dad.
Sorry for all the rude words.

And for Jo, who lovingly puts up with my
own fucking bad manners every day.

A BRIEF NOTE
ON SWEARING

There's a general rule in life that you shouldn't judge a book by its cover. In this case, however, you can probably make an exception, and you should use it as a pretty good guide to the contents. This is a book about good manners, with multiple uses of the word fucking (or variations thereof) dropped liberally throughout it. Four hundred and seventy-five uses, to be precise.

Swearing is considered impolite when broadcast in public, but whether it's acceptable does depend on the company you're in. Assuming that you've already read the title and it's piqued your interest enough to open it and read more, we'll assume you're OK with some potty language. If you're looking to learn about good manners and are likely to be offended by such words, then I would recommend any of the titles listed at the back in the fucking bibliography.

'As we look for new answers in the modern age, I for one prefer the tried and tested recipes, like speaking well of each other and respecting different points of view, coming together to seek out the common ground and never losing sight of the bigger picture.'

HM QUEEN ELIZABETH II,
24 JANUARY 2019

Rough translation:

'We need to learn some fucking good manners.'

CONTENTS

INTRODUCTION

❧

'The hardest job kids face today is learning
good manners without seeing any.'
FRED ASTAIRE

❧

A book on manners wouldn't hold much credibility without beginning with a thank you for buying it. If you didn't buy it, please pass on my sincere gratitude to whoever purchased it for you. If you're just browsing through a friend's toilet library, then thanks for selecting it over old copies of *National Geographic* and unread Christmas gifts. Please make sure you leave the room as you found it and wash your hands on the way out. If you've stolen it, well, perhaps reading it might help you see the error of your ways.

It's important to clarify straight away that this isn't a book about how to be posh. It's not something to refer to when you unexpectedly receive an invitation to Buckingham Palace or the White House.

It will be of little to no use if you're looking for pointers on how much to tip, nor will it enlighten you on the correct protocol for entering into courtship with a dignitary's offspring.

I've read numerous books that contain these 'gems' of wisdom and quickly discovered that, as useful as they once were, we've got some slightly bigger fucking issues to deal with these days. Society on both sides of the Atlantic feels more divided than it ever has, and in among all the confusion we've let our behaviour get a little out of control.

I'm in no way suggesting that lowering the volume of your music or letting someone into traffic are more important than finding a solution to reducing plastic waste or policies on national security. Just that we can't lower ourselves to the levels of screaming, shouting and stamping our feet about things, simply because we haven't got our way – that behaviour is reserved for humans under the age of five, the cast of *TOWIE* and anyone who's appeared on *The Apprentice*. Life isn't fucking fair, but we should be able to demonstrate our ability to get the basics right before we move on to the more complex stuff.

It's more difficult than it sounds. When dealing with such sensitive subjects it's extremely likely that emotions will run high, but we need to hold our heads equally high and maintain some dignity. The quick and easy response is to speak louder and more forcefully; the harder and more time-consuming way is to listen and understand the other side of the argument (and there's always another side), and use that to come to a sensible solution.

And there's part of the fucking problem: time. Manners have nothing to do with class or wealth – as so frequently demonstrated by a variety of overpaid public figures – they cost nothing, after all. But they do take time, and in our busy little bubbles that's almost more valuable than money. We're cash-rich and time-poor, so who gives a fuck if we offend a few people by cutting our nails on the train or pushing to the front of the queue? You'll probably never see those individuals again anyway. We've all got a million things to do and are constantly connected to other people doing a million other things, so the faster we can get things done the better, right? Well, wrong. The faster we get things done, the faster we get them done. The better way always takes a lot more time.

Another issue that's causing us some major fucking problems in the good manners department is our increasing connectivity with the rest of the world. Back in the hunter-gatherer days our contact with other humans would be limited to how far we could walk, but then we learned how to domesticate horses, and that number grew a little more. Fast forward a couple of thousand years and we've invented bicycles, cars, buses, trains and aeroplanes – machines that have the ability to take us to new countries and cultures in the time it takes to not watch a couple of Liam Neeson films. Add the online community to this and we're suddenly thrown together with thousands of people on a daily basis. It's simply not possible to be nice to all of them.

British anthropologist Robin Dunbar knows a thing or two about how many friends one person needs. That's why he wrote a book called *How Many Friends Does One Person Need?* His research into primates shows a direct correspondence between the size of the brain's neocortex (which deals with complex shit like high-order functions) and 'the number of people you can have a relationship with involving trust and obligation.'[1]

That number – now known as 'Dunbar's Number' – is 150. Compare that to the number of people you come into contact with on an average day – on the train, in the shops, in the toilets, in the *MailOnline* comments section – and you start to get an idea of exactly how many complete strangers our lives are filled with. Amy Alkon notes in her book *Good Manners For Nice People Who Sometimes Say F*ck*, 'We're experiencing more rudeness because we've lost the constraints on our behaviour that we've had in place for millions of years . . . You can behave terribly to strangers and have a good chance of getting away with it because you'll probably never see your victims again.'

Our brains simply aren't designed to cope with the scale of modern human interaction, so we shield ourselves away from these strangers, switch off our emotions and forget our fucking manners. As Graham Waters (Don Cheadle) says in 2004's *Crash*: 'We're always behind this metal and glass. I think we miss that touch so much, that we crash into each other just so we can feel something.'

We're also living in a world that increasingly blurs the lines between private and public, between formal and informal, and we've lost the ability to distinguish between the two. Whether it's a result of social media, journalism or whataboutism, a habit seems to be developing where what's acceptable in the home among friends, is also acceptable in public among complete fucking strangers. We pass off offensive comments in the workplace or on the street as friendly 'banter' (or bantz, as it's often known) when in fact it's just plain fucking rude. We've got office bantz and pub bantz and locker room bantz and sexist bantz and political bantz. I couldn't give a rat's arse about 'I am who I am', 'Be yourself', 'Just do it' or whatever pseudo-motivational sports shoe slogan you choose to live your life by, there's a time and a place for everything. How you behave with friends in private is a very fucking different thing to how you should conduct yourself in public.

Passing off offensive comments as banter is nothing new. Whether it's Chris Morris satirising paedophiles or suicide bombers, Frankie Boyle talking about the Paralympics, or Kathy Griffin holding up a severed head of Donald Trump, you'll always find someone, somewhere pushing the boundaries of decency.

Of course you can be funny without being rude, but a fairly large proportion of comedy is likely to be offensive in some way to someone, somewhere. There's normally a butt to every joke. Lenny Bruce, Andy Kaufman, Bill Hicks, Joan Rivers, Richard Pryor, Russell Brand, Michael Richards, Doug Stanhope, Kevin Hart, Sarah Silverman, Roseanne Barr and Jo Brand have all had their bottoms smacked publicly at some point for overstepping the mark on a number of subjects, including race, religion, suicide, sexuality, rape, 9/11 and throwing battery acid at politicians. It doesn't matter if you find these things hugely offensive or fucking hilarious, when they're held up as examples of what's funny, it's hardly surprising that their tone and sentiment is echoed on the streets. But it's their job to say controversial things; it's our job to recognise that we shouldn't repeat them in public. We need to learn to distinguish between our private and public lives, and recognise what's acceptable and where.

And that's exactly why I've found writing a book on fucking good manners a most troublesome task. There's simply no way of writing a whole book about how people should behave that will have readers across the world nodding their heads in agreement. For one, because in Bulgaria and other Baltic states people quite often shake their head from side to side to show agreement. Excessive eye contact is regarded as aggressive in Japan, but courteous in the US; crossing your fingers in Vietnam is a symbol for a vagina; a harmless thumbs up translates as 'fuck you' in parts of Greece and Iran. There is no global code of conduct, and even if you take away these perceived cultural quirks, a lot still depends on individual circumstances and opinion.

So what are we left with? Well, some of it's manners, some etiquette, some courtesy and general politeness, some anti-social behaviour, some laws of the land, some common-fucking-sense, and probably some plain old boring #firstworldproblems. But it's not meant to be a checklist of how everyone should behave on a daily basis. I'm not judging anyone who does any of these things – except, perhaps one or two of the celebrities mentioned for their diva behaviour. We've all been guilty of some fairly knobbish behaviour at some point in life, and let the crazy little voices inside our heads justify our reasons for doing so. This book is simply an attempt to highlight a few of these errors, and perhaps help us all look out for each other from time to time. With some potty words thrown in for dramatic effect. As Emily Post – the godmother of modern etiquette – said: 'Manners are a sensitive awareness of the feelings of others. If you have that awareness, you have good manners, no matter what fork you use.'[2]

∾

A HISTORY OF MANNERS

❧

*'Consideration for others is the basis
of a good life, a good society.'*

CONFUCIUS

❧

We might take for granted that much of what's perceived as acceptable behaviour in modern society is common-bloody-sense, but that hasn't always been the case. Just as manners change from one culture to another, so they have evolved over time as we attempt to become more and more civilised. Once upon a time it wasn't particularly frowned upon to be seen urinating in the dining room (master of the house only, not the servants), or eating with your hands, or using the skull of your enemy as a ceremonial drinking vessel. But some of us have moved on since then.

Perhaps the best place to start is around 1500 BC when a chap called Moses walked down a mountain with a few rules carved into stone. Ten, to be precise. Among some of the more fundamental ideas such as

No Stealing, No Murdering and No Adultery, we got a decent schooling on lying, coveting and honouring. A Good Book also reminds us all to 'Love thy neighbour as thyself.'

The Romans were keen to adopt a more civilised society and it was their Empire that introduced us to the early concept of the metrosexual, with baths, nasal trimming and toothbrushes demonstrating a consideration towards others. Sadly they were yet to invent toothpaste, so had to make do with a delicious mixture of crushed bones and horse urine, for long-lasting, pissy-fresh breath.

Horses also play an important role in the next big step, but not until the Middle Ages when the concept of chivalry became a bit of a thing. The word derives from the French *chevalier*, meaning horseman. These brave and noble knights in shining armour were famed for their heroic quests and ability to save princesses from people with dubious moral standards. On top of that it appears they were also more in touch with their emotions, and knew how to charm the ladies. A Code of Chivalry was created, the contents of which vary depending on who you're reading, but roughly speaking it gives a big thumbs up to respecting others, being brave, generous, loyal and honest, and not tethering your horse in a disabled bay.

Around a similar time a gentleman called Daniel of Beccles was creating what many consider to be the first modern book on manners: *Urbanus Magnus*, or *The Book of the Civilised Man*. It's a 3,000-line poem in Latin that covers three main themes: social hierarchy, self-control and sexual morality, dispensing such invaluable pointers as: 'do not attack your enemy while he is squatting to defecate', 'do not openly evacuate your nostril by twisting your fingers' and, if visiting a sex worker: 'empty your testicles quickly and depart quickly.'[3]

The 16th century saw a flurry of notable works from various parts of Europe, perhaps due to the increased thuggery on display across the continent. Erasmus of Rotterdam became the first person to lose his shit in public about kids of today not respecting their elders in *De Civilitate Morum Puerilium* (1530) (aka *A Handbook on Good Manners for Children*). And then Giovanni Della Casa penned *Galateo: The Rules of Polite Behaviour* in 1558 which gave some helpful advice on not bragging about your children, checking your mail in front of other people, or joking about disabilities, as well as further consideration on nasal etiquette: 'You do not want, when you blow your nose, to then open the hanky and gaze at your snot as if pearls or rubies might have descended from your brains.'[4]

In 1533 another Italian, Catherine de Medici, made a significant contribution to the mannersphere when she married Henry II of France. Along with the many other culinary delights she brought with her from Italy, she also packed a weird stick with prongs on it. This was a fork, and it soon caught on across the courts of France and the rest of Europe as a sign of refinement and sophistication. But it wasn't for another few hundred years that we'd start arguing over which one was for the fish, and which one was for the salad.

Around the middle of the 18th century, the 4th Earl of Chesterfield, Philip Stanhope (Phil to his mates), laid down some ground rules for his son on becoming a nice guy, including such life-affirming, timeless classics as 'Whatever's worth doing at all, is worth doing well', 'Never put off till tomorrow what you can do today' and 'Do as you would be done by, is the surest method of pleasing'.[5] Stanhope's words were never meant to be published, but *Letters to His Son on the Art of Becoming a Man of the World and a Gentleman* (1746–47) became an influential bestseller. It's also one of the first examples of the word etiquette being used in the modern English language, derived from the French *étiquette*, meaning label or small sign.

So the story goes, Louis XIV of France started to get a bit pissed off with the rowdy behaviour at his summer parties trashing his garden. As a result he created a collection of signs to advise guests on appropriate behaviour – Please keep off the grass, No pissing in the fountain, No football shirts or trainers. That sort of stuff. Hence the word étiquette became synonymous with good manners.

Moving into the early 20th century and further unrest across Europe meant we needed another proverbial kick up the backside, which came from the sharp boot of Emily Post with *Etiquette in Society, in Business, in Politics, and at Home* (1922). Post covers a lot of the traditional values: 'Elbows are never put on the table while one is eating', 'A lady never asks a gentleman to dance, or to go to supper with her' and 'To do exactly as your neighbours do is the only sensible rule'.[6] Which is fine, so long as you've never lived next to Fred and Rose West. She also, perhaps inadvertently, gave advice that many modern men – from Sir Ian Botham to Anthony Weiner – should take notice of:

'A gentleman does not boast about his junk.'

In 1936 Dale Carnegie released his bestseller *How To Win Friends And Influence People*, which could easily be seen as a book on courtesy, if only with a bit more of an agenda attached to it. The word courtesy derives from the French word *courtoisie* or 'of the court'. Back in the Middle Ages nobles had to work out a plan to get in the king's good books if they wanted to run his land. Steven Pinker in his book *The Better Angels of Our Nature* writes:

> 'The nobles had to change their marketing. They had to cultivate their manners, so as not to offend the king's minions . . . The manners appropriate for the court came to be called "courtly" manners or "courtesy". The etiquette guides, with their advice on where to place one's nasal mucus, originated as manuals for how to behave in the king's court.'[7]

Substitute the word 'king' for 'managing director' or 'chairman' and you can see how Carnegie's tome is as much about manners as it is about running a successful business. Whether you agree with the scruples behind his thinking is a different matter. We all have agendas in life, whether they're hidden or not, but expecting something in return for our manners is a dangerous line to take.

In 2014 China introduced a 'Social Credit Rating' across parts of the country where citizens are rated on their conduct and behaviour. Being good gives you privileges such as access to the best schools, discounts on energy bills and even boosted ratings on dating websites. Conversely, stepping out of line can result in a travel ban, restrictions on jobs and having your dog taken away. The programme is set for full roll-out across the country by 2020, under the catchy/creepy banner of 'keeping trust is glorious and breaking trust is disgraceful'.[8] It sounds like the kind of dystopian vision of the future dreamt up in the mind of George Orwell or Charlie Brooker, and in fact the latter's *Black Mirror* episode 'Nosedive' (2016) is pretty much a carbon copy of this Big Brother state.

Showing kindness and consideration towards others should only be done because it's a fucking kind and considerate thing to do. If something other than a warm glow of satisfaction comes out of it, then consider it an added bonus. As Giovanni Della Casa said back in 1558:

> 'Our manners are attractive when we regard others' pleasure and not our own delight.'

∾

1. BASIC MANNERS

❧

'Telling a lie is called wrong. Telling the truth is called right. Except when telling the truth is called bad manners and telling a lie is called polite.'

JUDITH VIORST, 'MANNERS'

❧

BASIC MANNERS

The basics of manners should be – I hope – fairly fucking basic to get to grips with. Over the years we should have all picked up a reasonable sense of right and wrong from our family, friends and teachers, plus a few pointers from daytime television shows of a dubious moral nature. Whether we choose to put these principles into action on a regular basis is a little less fucking clear-cut.

Once we step outside our front door to go about our daily chores, we need to be aware that we're entering a shared space that's for all of us to use. Every day we encounter thousands of people, whether we're sat on the bus, in the office, or waiting in a queue for an *X-Factor* audition, and every day we experience thousands of tiny interactions with them. Most of these interactions will go largely unnoticed, but a lack of fucking good manners or a display of fucking bad manners can cause these insignificant moments to flare up into something altogether more troublesome. As such, good manners – no matter how basic they seem – provide an oil to our lives and allow us to navigate our days without friction. In *Time Enough For Love*, Robert A. Heinlein (aka the Dean of Science Fiction) writes:

'Moving parts in rubbing contact require lubrication to avoid excessive wear. Honorifics and formal politeness provide lubrication where people rub together. Often the very young, the untraveled, the naïve, the unsophisticated deplore these formalities as "empty," "meaningless," or "dishonest," and scorn to use them. No matter how "pure" their motives, they thereby throw sand into machinery that does not work too well at best.'[9]

Yes, it's a sci-fi novel and not exactly Socrates (philosopher, not legendary Brazilian attacking midfielder) but he makes a good point. We need something to ease us through our days and prevent ugly crashes with random strangers. We need to demonstrate an awareness of other people and be mindful of how we can help make their day run that bit smoother. Don't expect hugs, high fives or thank you cards in return, but a display of thoughtfulness could at least prevent a shit day from getting even shittier.

Manners are, obviously, very different from law, and you're under no legal obligation to help someone reach a can of sweetcorn off the top shelf, nor are you likely to be arrested for failing to hold a door open. However, we have to get to fucking grips with the fact that we share this planet with 7.7 billion other people, a large proportion of whom are just trying to get by without fucking up too badly. We're all in the same boat trying to do our best to keep a roof over our heads, and provide for our families, and get everything done so we can have half an hour to put our fucking feet up. And in order for everything to work smoothly – in order to help ourselves – we need to start by helping each other.

It's not a perfect system – as with any ideology there will always be some arsehat who takes advantage of it and feels they can do what the fuck they like. There'll always be some massive dick/jerk-wad/dipshit who believes the world revolves around them and everyone else is merely on this planet to help them get to the top. This is something we have to just take on the chin and accept as part of life. They may even make it to the top one day (or whatever/wherever they believe the top to be), and as human beings we'll naturally all do our best to fake sympathy when the giant cuntosaurus comes crashing back down to earth.

We all have our own reasons for the way we act towards others, from delusions of grandeur and narcissism to the tried-and-tested celebrity excuse of having 'a severe and unexpected reaction to prescribed medication', but there are some day-to-day basics that we should try and get right if we're all going to get along together. I'm not trying to teach anyone – or their grandparents – to suck eggs, just ticking off the obvious stuff before we delve into the more murky areas.

∼

Say please and thank you

This is where it all begins. An ever-so-basic under-standing that the vast majority of us rely on others to help us through our day, and the price of this is just a few simple words. It makes no difference if you're the head of an international business or an assist-ant in a print production company in Plymouth: if you need someone's help, say Please; if someone helps you, say Thank You. The Pleases don't always have to be pretty or come with a fucking cherry on top; the Thank Yous don't have to be accompan-ied by hugs and tears and speeches that would have Gwyneth Paltrow glancing at her watch.

We need to have the humility to acknowledge that we don't achieve everything by ourselves, and we aren't entitled to have everything we want. By saying Please we show some respect towards other people's time, and by saying Thank You we show some appreciation towards their possibly insignificant deed, and hopefully encourage them to continue doing more of That Good Thing. It costs nothing but the benefits are priceless.

(Please note that sending a text message on behalf of your kids when they receive a birthday present, doesn't count as an official thank you. Give them a fucking pen and some paper and help them understand the value of what they've been given.)

∽

Learn to fucking apologise

Hot on the tails of Please and Thank You comes Sorry. Some people (not just Elton John) have a big issue with saying the word, possibly for fear of liability (see chapter on driving) but saying Sorry should be a basic human response for when we fuck up.

We all make mistakes, but exactly who's at fault for these mistakes is often more up for debate, whether it's a clashing of shoulders on a busy street or the mis-selling of a pension fund. Countless generations of leading business figures and politicians refuse to use the word in case it results in them having to sell their eighteen-bedroom home in Hertfordshire, but there comes a point when you should really hold your fucking hands up. People are actively trained to avoid using the word for fear of legal obligations, instead resorting to shitwad nonpologies such as 'It is an unfortunate situation' or 'It is regrettable'.

On the flipside of it all we have the willingness of the other party to forgive. This is more closely linked to the nature and severity of the crime: an apology for driving under the influence and claiming the Jewish community are responsible for all world wars, might be harder to accept than one for rubbing sandpaper on a cricket ball and then trying to hide the offending item in your jockstrap.

Whatever your crime, saying Sorry is always the first step to finding a solution.

∾

Hold the fucking door

Many people live by the somewhat muddled concept that respect is something that should be earned – that you have to do something impressive or world-changing for people to respect you. For those people I have four words: Get. A. Fucking. Grip. The default setting for all human beings should be to give respect first. It doesn't mean that you have to become friends on Facebook, or start a crochet club or go camping in the Cotswolds together. It just means that when we meet complete strangers we do basic helpful things, like hold doors open and give them a hand with heavy bags, to demonstrate that we're a human-fucking-being too. It shouldn't matter how old or young they are, what gender they are or what football shirt they're wearing, if you walk through a door, your first instinct should be to look behind you and check if someone else is following. If they are, then take a fraction of a second to hold the door rather than let it slam in their fucking face.

～

Mind your fucking personal habits

We all have our own quirky/weird/fucking irritating habits that we do almost without thinking. For some it might be drumming your fingers when you're pressed for time, or constantly clicking your pen when you're deep in thought, or whistling 1980s' power ballads when you're doing a crossword. Others might have slightly more objectionable habits such as plucking their eyebrows, or constantly sniffing, or doing some nose-gardening with their finger. These are personal habits and not hurting anyone if they're kept personal – leave it up to your parents/partner/kids to call you out for being gross. But do be aware that performing such personal habits in public may not be met with the same level of tolerance and forgiveness as demonstrated by your nearest and dearest. Sitting on a train for two hours stuck next to someone who's sniffing every 30 seconds can be perceived as a form of modern torture, so things can get most unpleasant if your neighbour eventually cracks.

∽

Don't fucking interrupt

We seem to have become very good talkers in recent years – perhaps a result of us having a universe of knowledge available at the touch of a button. Everyone's within a few clicks of becoming a fucking expert in something, and all too happy to share their opinion of global trade deals or quantum physics based on a radio show they heard while shampooing the dog. The problem is that our desire to express an opinion is equally matched by our ability to talk over the top of someone else's. I've gone into a bit more depth about interrupting in the chapter on workplace manners (Chapter 10), but the gist of it is that we need to learn to listen before we start to fucking transmit.

∽

Learn some fucking table manners

Don't eat with your fingers. Don't put your elbows on the table. Don't speak with your mouth full.

Don't slurp your soup. Don't lick your plate. Don't stretch across people. Don't use the wrong fork. Don't slouch in your chair. Don't chew with your mouth open. Don't burp. Don't fart. Don't ask for seconds before others have finished their first helping. Don't shout. Don't tip your chair. Don't lick your knife. Don't put crumbs in the butter. Don't hold your knife like a pen. Don't talk about religion or politics. Don't pick your teeth. Don't double-dip your crudités. Don't eat your food too quickly. Don't eat it too slowly. Don't put your phone on the table. Etc., etc.

Or – if you prefer – do all of these things. Just do them in the privacy of your own fucking home. Perhaps when you don't have guests over. There are many long and helpful lists of table manners online, covering things like napkin folding and how to leave your cutlery once you've finished. Exactly how many of these suggestions you observe at your own dinner table are for you to decide, but when you're under the watchful eye of others then neglecting some – or all – of these things might be frowned upon. Or get you kicked out before you've sampled the amuse-bouche. Adapt your table manners to match the company you're in (royalty, board of directors, the posh folk down the road, friends, family, pets, etc.) and you should survive any unfortunate incidents.

~

Don't be fucking late

The ability to turn up when requested isn't quite as straightforward as it used to be. Arriving late became a trendy thing to do for a while, as well as a convenient excuse to jam in a few extra chores at home before you set off. Each individual scenario has its own set of nuances, depending on whether you're invited to someone's home, out for a cup of coffee, a restaurant, a meal with clients, or a meeting with Piers Morgan. You need to balance the consequences and potential distress/offence caused to your date/hosts/clients/co-workers by arriving late, with the importance of finishing whatever it is you're doing. But as a rule, don't be fucking late.

~

Put your fucking phone away

You'll notice this is a common theme throughout this book. I'm not anti-phones by any means, it just feels like we've lost all conception of what role they should play in our lives. They give us the power to find any fact, watch any film, listen to any song, read any book, control the heating, pay our bills, track our steps, check the weather, build new worlds and send photos of intimate body parts to loved ones thousands of miles away.

But the more power we have at our disposal, the more we need to demonstrate some fucking responsibility. We need to disconnect with all this power to reconnect with the world around us. Put your fucking phone away, turn it off and just focus on one thing at a time.

Once you're done, sure – get back to checking how many fucking steps you've taken today or playing *Candy Crush* or whatever. Just don't let it get in the way of everything else you should be doing.

❧

Keep your fucking mouth shut

Perhaps one of the most difficult of modern manners to get to grips with is learning when to bite our tongues and shut the fuck up. We all like to think that our opinions are intelligent/witty/thoughtful/ righteous, but that doesn't mean you need to wade into every single fucking injustice that you read about. Social media means we're only a couple of clicks away from finding someone, somewhere fighting every battle, but for fuck's sake just leave it alone. Talk about it with your friends in the pub by all means – people who genuinely care about what you think – but don't get involved. Take a deep fucking breath and remember the words of H. Jackson Brown, Jr.:

> 'Good manners sometimes means simply putting up with other people's bad manners.'

(Also, see Chapter 12 on social media.)

∼

2. PUBLIC TRANSPORT

❧

*'I have found out that there ain't no surer
way to find out whether you like people or
hate them than to travel with them.'*

Mark Twain, *Tom Sawyer Abroad*

❧

PUBLIC TRANSPORT

Public transport – be it by plane, train, bus or boat – is considered by many to be the Wild West of the manners world. There are few other places on this planet where we find so many people crammed together in such a small space, each one rushing to their destination to meet that essential deadline, each one with their own unique sense of self-importance. People who are on their way to work, or coming home from a football match, or who have been drinking in the park all day; people who have suddenly noticed their nails are a bit long, or their eyebrows are overgrown, or need to shave before a job interview; people who have just been fired from their job for lewd behaviour, or are visiting from Russia to see the magnificent beauty of Salisbury Cathedral.

All these not-so-bright-or-beautiful people of all different ages, from all different cultures and backgrounds, each with their own individual idea of what constitutes good and bad manners, swarming through train stations, airports and subways every day. It's no wonder they become flashpoints for petty arguments, heavy tutting and exaggerated eye-rolling. It's no wonder temperatures both literal and figurative can run so high, and the tiniest of sparks – a faint but irritating disco beat from some headphones; an old lady fumbling for the correct change in her purse; a cheesy waft of burger with extra gherkins – can explode into horrific battle-fields of name calling and finger pointing.

Transport used to be a place of such civility, where newspapers were occasionally ruffled and eyebrows raised in disapproval. But today people seem to have no qualms about bringing their pri-vate lives onto public transport, either through the detailed analysis of a partner's medical symptoms on the phone, or via a drunken copulation on the back seat of a bus (or under a blanket at 35,000 feet).

Even with helpful reminders being made every 30 seconds ('Please move right down inside the carriages', 'Please allow passengers off the train first', 'Please refrain from letting your two year old kick the shit out of the seat in front') it seems many people forget their manners the moment they enter a shared space with a group of strangers. Or more likely, ignored – let's face it, the chances of bumping into any of these people again once you're through passport control are fairly minimal. But just in case there's any doubt, let's make this as clear as fucking possible for everyone: public transport is a public place to be shared with other members of the public.

❧

A quick search of 'Plane rage' on YouTube brings up several million results with such catchy titles as 'Best of plane/airport freakouts 2017 compilation', 'Midflight meltdowns and airport a-holes', 'Pissed woman on my plane gets crazy' and 'Rage on plane, bride-to-be batters one of her hen party'. Not only is this proof of the heightened tension people feel on public transport these days, but also goes to show that when people do forget their manners/lose their shit in public, the first thing someone does is start filming it (see chapter on social media).

But of course it's not just regular folk who lack the ability to get from A to B without the slightest bit of TLC. Some of the big names in the celebrity world (but more regularly the slightly smaller ones) have managed to confuse the concept of public transport with private jets/limos, and thrown all manner of childish pissyfits at the suggestion that they start behaving themselves. A few examples include:

Snoop Dogg – part of a 30-strong brawl in London Heathrow after he was allegedly refused entry to the VIP lounge. The whole fracas was witnessed from the lounge by Ronan Keating, who apparently decided the best course of action was to say nothing at all.

Naomi Campbell – supermodel has strop. Hardly news, but Miss Campbell was booted off a BA flight to LA in 2008, then assaulted the police officer who came to escort her off.

Ivana Trump – allegedly got so mad on a flight in 2009 that she swore at a baby. Nowhere does it say if the baby's name was Donald.

Gérard Depardieu – desperate for a wee during take-off, he allegedly peed in a bottle and spilt some on the floor. The plane was grounded while they cleaned the carpet and the jovial Frenchman was told to book another flight. (And presumably reminded to always have a wee before setting off.)

Alec Baldwin – the *30 Rock* star was escorted from a flight after a war of words with a flight attendant, ironically over the app *Words With Friends*.

Ian Brown – perhaps the most disturbing case of celebrity air-rage came from the Stone Roses frontman, who apparently threatened to chop off the hands of an air stewardess who offered him the chance to browse Duty Free. Brown was jailed for four months, released after two.

~

Manners and public transport are a problem that's only getting worse as we have more commuters, more train journeys, more flights, more meetings and more important places to be. The main thing when on your journey is to remember that:

a)   Everyone's in the same boat/train/bus/ plane as you are.

b)   Losing your shit will <u>never</u> result in getting there any quicker.

You don't have to be on your best behaviour by any means, but there are some basic things you can do correctly to help everything run smoothly for everyone, the number one rule being:

∾

Keep your fucking cool

Just close your eyes, take a deep breath and remind yourself that you will eventually reach your destination and whoever/whatever's driving you up the fucking wall will soon be gone. If this is genuinely impossible and you have to say something then please proceed with caution, civility and perhaps an iPhone to submit as future evidence in the courtroom.

Here are a few other pointers to help your journey go as smoothly as possible, in no particular order of importance:

❧

Walk in a straight fucking line

This, apparently, is harder than you'd think for some, normally because they're attempting to play *Mega Dead Pixel* while navigating the underground system in rush hour. Get your head up, look where you're fucking going, and stick to the correct side, which is normally the same as the side you drive on (i.e. the left for the UK and Australia, and the right for the US).

❧

Stand on the fucking right

Most escalators – but not all – have enough space for two people to stand side by side. This doesn't mean that two people should stand side by side. One side is for those who want to stand, allowing space on the other for the busy folk who are sprinting to catch their train. Bags and suitcases should be kept directly in front of or behind you. If this isn't possible then you'll just have to prepare yourself for the inevitable onslaught of twatish comments from regular commuters, who'd never dare do something so disgracefully selfish. Ever.

❧

Have your fucking money ready

For those buses that still require you to use old-fashioned coins, do everyone a massive fucking favour and get your money ready. It doesn't have to be the precise change – we're not trying to achieve perfection – but you could at least spend the ten minutes you've been waiting at the bus stop to locate your purse from the infinite depths of your bag.

∾

Get out of the fucking way

Stations and airports are busy places, with millions passing through them every day. Some people know exactly where they're going, and some people don't. There's nothing wrong with that. However, should you find yourself in a busy place without the faintest clue of which direction to go in, please avoid standing at the top or bottom of the fucking escalator while you consider your options. Other incorrect places to stand/loiter/chat with friends include, but are not limited to: doorways of any kind and supermarket aisles. Just move to the side and find a quiet spot that doesn't have thousands of people trying to pass through it.

∾

Learn how to fucking queue

See Chapter 7.

❧

Turn your fucking music down

Yes. People have the right to listen to music on the bus. And the train. And the subway. But no one should feel the need to share their love of Chesney Hawkes with everyone else around them. You are not the one-and-fucking-only – there are others around you who were perfectly happy until you got on. Get some decent headphones. If you can't afford some, put them on your birthday or Christmas list. If you don't celebrate birthdays or Christmas then find another religious or cultural event that celebrates with the sharing of material gifts. Or just turn the fucking volume down.

If you're in any doubt as to whether others can hear your poor taste in music, take this simple test:

Step 1: Take your headphones out of your ears.
Step 2: Hold them at arm's length.
Step 3: Press play on your electronic audio device.
Step 4: If you can hear the music, it's too fucking loud.

Step 5: If you can't hear the music, it's
O-fucking-K.

❧

Put your fucking phone on silent

Of course, there are plenty of good reasons to be
using your mobile while travelling, so if you have
to, be sure to do it with the consideration of others,
whether you're in the designated 'Quiet Coach' or
not. Turn your ringtone off, keep your voice down,
keep your calls short, and if you do need to discuss
the possibility that Darren has herpes, then . . .
then . . . Do it via text? Or go and talk face-to-face.
Or call from the privacy of your own fucking home.

❧

Keep your fucking voice down

It's not just phone conversations that can cause small
vessels in your forehead to spontaneously erupt.
Being stuck next to a group of people (normally hen/
stag dos or LADZ on the way to a footie game) can
be equally fucking irritating, especially if they decide
to include you in their hilarious banter. Please just
accept that some people are perfectly fucking happy
not discussing the intricacies of vegan sausage rolls
or joining in with your homophobic footie songs.

෴

Take your fucking bags off the seat

The luggage racks are for putting your luggage on, the chairs are for putting your arse on. There should be no confusion on this matter. Be aware of the rough passenger-to-empty-seat ratio on your vehicle and move your fucking bag when it's busy, before someone has to ask you to. If you forget and someone asks to sit where your bag is, try smiling politely and saying 'Sorry, no problem', rather than huffing about like someone's asked you to lick a badger's arsehole.

෴

Take your fucking rucksack off

This may seem like it only applies to students and backpackers, but increasingly commuters appear to be unable to leave the house without looking like they're heading to base camp at Everest. Upon entering the carriage, please remove your rucksack and hold it by your feet. It means that during busy hours more people can get on, and during less busy hours you won't accidentally smack the person behind you in the face.

෴

Move down inside the fucking carriage

Yes, you know who you are. And yes, you're worried you might not be able to get off at your stop. But you will, so pretty please, move the fuck down.

❧

Take your fucking litter with you

Just because someone's being paid to clean the carriages after you leave, it doesn't mean you have to test their ability by using the sides of your seat as a trash can. If you brought the rubbish on, take it off as well, or at the very least put it all in a bag so someone else can bin it easily.

❧

Don't act like a fucking idiot

In recent years the rise of stag and hen dos heading to foreign soils has rocketed, which means budget airlines are normally half full/empty of noisy and utterly hilarious people, who have been drinking since 6am to make up for the fact they're not really having that much fun. I've no real objection to drinking on planes or trains, but do everyone a fucking favour and show some consideration towards the other 300 passengers.

❧

Keep your fucking legs closed

Underground, overground or at 35,000 feet, the width of the seat is a good indicator as to the maximum space your legs should take up. No one's got such enormous bollocks that their knees should encroach into their neighbour's zone, so quit the manspreading and keep your fucking legs together. If the carriage is generally empty then sure – feel free to spread out a little, but keep them together at all other times.

Armrests are a completely different matter and generally operate under the rule of first come, first served. However, as most planes have rows of three, a more considerate gesture is to give the person sat in the middle priority for their elbows. But it's not the law.

$\sim$

Watch what you're fucking watching

Some people mistakenly think trains are a private place, and as such they have a right to watch whatever uber-violent, semi-pornographic Netflix series they like. Wrong. If your screen's visible to others it's up to you to make sure it's appropriate. No one's going to object to being subjected to the scene where Bambi's mother's shot, but you'll just have to wait

until you get home to watch the latest episode of
Game of Thrones or *Life After Porn*.

∾

Stand clear of the fucking doors

Let. People. Off. Before. You. Get. On. It's painfully
simple, blindingly obvious, head-against-a-brick-
wall-ingly-basic common sense. In the same way it
makes sense to wait for your faecal matter to stop
coming out of your arse before you attempt to wipe
it. Just wait calmly until everyone's off, perhaps
even offering a polite hand to anyone who looks like
they might need a bit of assistance minding the gap.
There's a good citizen.

∾

Keep your fucking socks/shoes on

Feet are generally considered one of the more unpleasant areas of the body, purely from an olfactory
point of view. Flying tends to increase the blood pressure in your feet, which is why removing your shoes
on planes is not such an unreasonable act, provided
you've got some relatively clean socks available, and
you don't try and poke your feet through to the seat
in front. If you want to pop your long-haul flight
socks on, fine, but no one wants to have your naked,

stinking, blistered, fungal-infected, bunion-ed, verruca-ed feet on display anywhere near them. Take some joy from the fact your mild discomfort is really doing everyone else a massive fucking favour. Any sort of shoe-removal on trains is not acceptable.

❧

Personal fucking hygiene

It may provide you with an extra half an hour in bed in the morning, or give you something to pass the time, but trains and buses are not beauty salons to apply/remove make-up on. A quick top up of lipstick? Probably OK, maybe a little eye-liner too, but anything that smells bad (nail polish or remover) or requires its own specialist lighting system should be left at home. Your choices are simple: get up earlier or use a bathroom. But don't make the whole carriage suffer your puckering and plucking. Please note – there is never, ever, any fucking excuse for using an electric razor or cutting your fingernails on public transport.

❧

Recline your fucking seat gently

Once the signal has been given on a plane that the captain is happy for everyone to undo their seatbelts and recline their seats, don't instantly hit the button and smash it back as fast as you fucking can. There's a person behind you. Possibly with their head forward, or ridiculously long legs, or a drink or a baby in their hand. Or both. Just take it nice and easy, perhaps even signalling your intentions by dropping it a centimetre or so before pausing briefly and continuing the rest of the way. If you're feeling particularly considerate you might even warn them that you're about to recline your seat, but there's no need to actually ask permission.

~

Get a fucking room

Public Displays of Affection (PDAs) that are acceptable on public transport include: holding hands, a hug, a kiss of no more than one second. Winking is also fine. (That's with an *i*, not an *a*.) Anything more than this really has no place in public, at 35,000 feet above the Atlantic or 250 feet below the English Channel. It doesn't matter how much you're in love, or how long it is before you'll see each other again, or how much you've had to drink, keep it in the fucking bedroom.

~

Get your own fucking book

Should the situation arise where you find your-self without any form of entertainment to pass the time on your travels, please don't resort to reading over your fellow passenger's shoulder. A glance at a newspaper headline is fine, but anything more than that becomes a distraction to them, no matter how subtle you think you're being about it.

❧

Let them fucking out

You can almost guarantee that the moment you get comfy on a flight is the same moment the person next to you needs to get up for a piss. As annoying as this may be, the chances are they're probably not doing it on purpose, and it's less disruptive than sitting next to someone who's pissed themselves. You can avoid the quandary of 'crotch or arse?'* by simply standing up and letting them out, rather than grimacing and moving your legs six inches. If you're the one attempting to get out then use the time to retrieve anything you need from the overhead storage while you're up, so you're not asking them to move every twenty fucking seconds.

* Crotch is generally considered more polite if you do have to squeeze past.

✍

Give up your fucking seat

Another simple rule that seems to have been lost/
forgotten/ignored. If you see someone on the bus or
train who you think might be struggling to stand,
regardless of their age or gender, then offer them
your seat. It's not about chivalry or being old fash-
ioned or sexist or anything other than IT'S JUST
A POLITE FUCKING THING TO DO. You
don't have to announce it to the whole carriage or
make a deal out of the fact that other people haven't
given up their seats, just catch their eye and make
the international gesture for 'would you like to sit
down?' (Which is sort of like a semi-crouch, with
raised eyebrows and finger pointing to your seat.
Be sure to make sure you're definitely pointing to
the seat and not another body part.) And conversely,
if someone does offer you their seat, and you're not
really that old, or that pregnant (or pregnant at all),
then just decline it politely. They're just being nice
and looking out for others, so don't get your fucking
knickers in a twist about it.

✍

Mind your fucking table manners

It is your duty as a commuter to share any table space equally among those sat at the table. There's no 'first come first served' rule that entitles you to spread your laptop out across the table, along with your takeaway coffee, breakfast roll, newspaper, umbrella, gloves and portable printer. Feel free to expand into the space if no one's sat opposite you, but once someone sits down an equal percentage of that table space becomes their rightful property. If you use some fucking manners and ask politely, they might even let you share it.

∾

Stay behind the fucking line

There's a line on the floor that runs around the edge of the airport baggage carousel. Nearby there are signs with the words 'Please stand behind the line when waiting for your bags' written on them. That applies to you, your trolley and your mildly obnoxious kid who's sticking his fingers in the belt and everyone's watching and bracing themselves for a nasty accident, but ultimately won't do anything because it's your kid and you should be fucking looking after it. Thanks.

3. DRIVING

❧

*'Have you ever noticed that anybody
driving slower than you is an idiot and
anyone going faster is a maniac?'*
GEORGE CARLIN

❧

DRIVING

There's something odd that happens when a person gets behind the wheel of a car. Perfectly normal, rational-minded, community-spirited people turn into lip-chewing, nostril-flaring, fist-waving, bird-flipping dickwads. There are many possible reasons for this – the precious nature of time, increased stress in people's lives, bigger, more powerful cars and perhaps a deep, subconscious insecurity that stems from their feeling unloved by their father.

One thing's for sure, there are definitely more cars on the road than ever before, and more cars mean more chance that you'll bump into one of the aforementioned dickwads. Over the last 60 years the number of cars on the UK's roads has grown from 4.2 million to 38.4 million, and over 80 per cent of these drivers have experienced some form of road rage.[10]

The main cause of road rage (it's all over the front page) comes from a combination of:

a) People thinking they're fucking good drivers.
b) Other people thinking they're better fucking drivers.

Both parties are wrong.

Everyone makes mistakes when driving – finding themselves in the wrong lane, forgetting to indicate – but few are prepared to forgive people for it. It gives us a perverse sense of superiority to point out other people's mistakes, but no good ever comes of it. Add to that a number of factors – size, make, model and cost of car, how late you're running and how severe the accident-that-never-happened could have been – and things kick off in a most ugly manner. If you're lucky it's an exchange of hand signals and naughty words, if you're not so lucky things get physical and people get hurt.

In the UK it's a completely made up set of facts that Audi drivers make the rudest drivers, with over 84 per cent of people not-surveyed saying they had been cut up, tailgated or not thanked by the smug twats in the last 30 minutes. In fact, there's a small single-lane street on the outskirts of Hemel Hempstead where two Audi Q7 drivers have been stuck for the last eighteen months waiting for the other to give way to them. But a more legitimate survey (OK, one conducted by TV channel Dave) showed it's not too far from the truth. Their top five rudest car owners list reads:

1. BMW M3

2. Range Rover
3. Audi TT
4. Mercedes-Benz C-Class
5. Ford Transit Van

The problem is that no matter how good a driver you are – or think you are – shit will always happen. People will always lose their way, end up in the wrong lane, drive too slowly, or too fast. There'll always be someone who's late for work, or passing a rice cake to a screaming toddler in the back seat, or trying to retrieve their e-cig from the glove box, or screaming aggressively at another Brexit debate on their radio.

Plus, cars are no longer simply a means of transport to get from A to B – they come complete with entertainment units, navigation devices, hands-free kits, climate control systems, motorised baby-changing stations and popcorn machines. All designed to make our car-driving experience as leisurely as possible, when in actual fact they just distract us from the job we're meant to be doing (driving), much to the frustration of everyone else on the road. It all results in angry, distracted people who refuse to accept they've done anything wrong, and a fucking massive carpet of red mist descends over everyone.

The Highway Code gives us plenty of guidance on the rules of the road, but few people tend to read the thing once they've ripped up their L plates. More often it's our own made-up, social rules that cause the problems. Driving in the countryside, where there's less traffic and people generally have a bit more time on their hands, is different to driving in a big city centre. The former tends to be a bit more relaxed (or dithery, depending on your viewpoint), the latter a bit more forceful (or twatish, if you prefer). But as we drive merrily around the roads, studiously checking our mirrors and observing the speed limit, we need to remember that when things go wrong we have a simple choice to make:

a) Fly into a rage and gesticulate wildly, using varying degrees of unofficial international sign language.
b) Smile and wave.

Option a) is easy and guaranteed to make you feel better for approximately 0.35 seconds, followed by a sense of bitter self-loathing and possible escalated violence. Option b) is a bit harder to train your brain to do, but generally comes with longer-term happiness and emotional fulfilment.

Road rage is the disease, but like Sylvester Stallone, you can be the cure. Sly's weapons of choice were mirror shades, some form of automatic weapon with laser sighting and a chewed matchstick. Your weapons are your manners – set them to full power.

Wherever you're driving – no matter how badly you were cut up or infuriated by someone else's lack of manners, the most important rule of road etiquette is to let the dickwads be dickwads. If you're genuinely concerned then make a note of the registration and let the police know about it, but don't lower yourself to their level, or attempt to converse with them about the finer points of the Highway Code. Swallow any sense of injustice and get on with going where you're going. You never know what grade of dickwad could be behind the wheel, what kind of day they've had, or what level of insecurity they're suffering from after being teased in the showers 40 years ago. It could be a drunk-driving crossbow-wielding nut, a martial arts enthusiast who's just discovered his wife's been cheating on him, or it could be Hull's very own anti-hero Ronnie fucking Pickering (see YouTube for more details).

But in the interests of general happiness and road harmony across the world, here are some other fucking good manners to consider:

❧

Get out of the fucking middle lane

Motorways have different lanes for different things. One (the left one in the UK and Australia, right in the US) is for general driving. The next one over is for overtaking. The one next to that is for overtaking the overtakers. Once you've finished overtaking, move back into the fucking left-hand lane. Yes, you may well argue that you're overtaking a lorry that's two miles ahead, or that there's an extra lane on motorways if people want to get past, but FFS just get out of the middle lane.

❧

Leave a sensible fucking gap

In some people's minds, driving within two feet of a car's rear bumper at 70 miles per hour is an effective way of communicating to them to move over and let you past. While this may well have the desired effect, it also causes the driver in front to shit their pants, and shitting your pants is not something you want to happen when driving at 70 miles per hour. Just have some fucking patience, give people some space and they'll move over eventually.

❧

Don't be so fucking pushy

City drivers tend to be a little more forceful when pulling out at a junction, and that's to be expected. When you've got ten times the number of cars on the road you need to be a bit more assertive, but there is a more polite way of edging out into traffic that doesn't involve a smug sense of entitlement – a respectful crawl until some kind-hearted person eventually flashes their lights to let you in. If you're behind a car that's been let out at a junction, please resist the urge to take the crown of King Twat by pushing out bumper to bumper with them. Just wait your fucking turn.

❧

Learn how to fucking park (part 1)

There are nice, white lines neatly marked in most car parks, and the aim of the game is to position your car between these lines, allowing for the maximum number of people to park. Many of these car parks have redrawn these lines to accommodate the growing number of wider vehicles, or perhaps just to give drivers a bit more room to squeeze out of their doors. If you're worried about your top-of-the-range luxury crossover being scratched then use one of these spaces, but don't take the misguided view that you can simply use two regular spots if none are available. Find somewhere else (or perhaps invest in a smaller car?) and don't kid yourself into thinking that paying for two tickets entitles you to park in two spaces.

~

Let someone out

Not everyone. Just one car every couple of minutes to keep things rolling and pass on some positivity. Just as road rage is contagious, so is kindness, and by letting one person out it will hopefully encourage them to do the same to someone else. Thus these insignificant moments of altruism ripple out across the land like magical butterflies of happiness.

~

Say thank you

Following the most joyous show of public courtesy outlined above – or any other act of thoughtfulness – it's essential that it's acknowledged by the driver in one way or another. This could be a cheery wave of the hand, a thumbs up or flashing your hazard lights as you drive away. Failure to do so puts you on the same list of utter shitwads as Jordan Belfort and the guy with the shiny teeth who tried to organise a festival for posh kids in the Bahamas.

Sometimes it's nice to wave a hand in return as a gesture of 'No problem', but subsequent communication is not required. It's simply a matter of making other people on the road feel like human beings, rather than a source of irritation getting in your fucking way.

❧

Hold your fucking hands up

Just like saying thanks, we need to hold our literal and figurative hands up if we screw up. The problem is that for generations we've been told never to apologise for anything on the road, because that's accepting liability, and accepting liability means you're at fault, and being at fault means a fucking massive premium on next year's insurance. So what you say in the event of an actual accident is up to you. But should you pull out a bit late and cut someone up or accidentally drift out of your lane on a roundabout or get a bit too close to a cyclist, just hold your hand up and say sorry. So long as no one's hurt, we'll all be OK. Please make sure when you hold your hand up that all five digits are held up too and not just the middle one.

❧

Learn how to fucking park (part 2)

Disabled spots are for people who have more difficulty getting access to shops and venues. Just because you've got so much money that you wipe your arse with paper worth more than the fixed penalty, it doesn't mean you can park there. Yes, I'm looking at you John Terry, George Osborne, Victoria Beckham, Miley Cyrus, Kanye, Britney and Usher (to name just a few). Be grateful that you have the ability to walk long distances and leave the spaces free for someone who genuinely fucking needs them. Similarly, family bays are technically reserved for adults with children under the age of twelve (in the UK), but leaving them for parents who genuinely need them (with children under the age of five, for example) is a much more considerate thing to do.

∽

Look out for cyclists

The battle between drivers and cyclists is a long and brutal one, sadly with casualties on both sides. We haven't got space here to delve into all the details, but it's important to point out that in a collision between the two modes of transport, it's normally the cyclists who end up second best. This alone should

be enough to make sure that no matter how infuri-
ating a cyclist's behaviour may be, no matter how
wrong they are, put their safety first. And on the
flipside, cyclists: do take a bit of extra fucking care.

∼

Give yourself more time

The majority of fuckwitish behaviour on our roads
is a result of simply not leaving enough time for the
journey. Speeding, tailgating, cutting people up and
parking like a twat all come from trying to leave
everything to the last minute, turning our cars into
apparently acceptable places to eat breakfast, have
a shave or draw on our eyebrows. We need to stop
trying to micromanage every millisecond of our lives
and treat ourselves to the luxury of arriving early.
Try it once in a while – you might like it.

∼

Learn how to fucking indicate

If you need to turn across traffic at the lights (right
in the UK and Australia, left in the US) and there is
no separate filter lane, then indicate that you need
to turn right before you get to the fucking lights.
This allows the cars behind you to move into the
other lane and drive past. Don't wait until the lights

change and then start signalling, because everyone else gets fucking stuck behind you.

∾

Put your fucking phone away

It's the law, of course, but that doesn't stop thousands of people taking a quick peek at a text message, or loading a playlist, or answering it really quickly and putting it on speakerphone next to you. Just put the fucking thing away and everyone will be fine. Seriously. The only thing you'll miss out on is a hefty fine and six points on your licence. And yes – everyone can see your eyes flitting up and down between the road and the phone on your lap. We all know what you're doing.

∾

Turn your fucking music down

Yes that's right, Dawg. You, driving around town trying to intimidate old people with your gangster rap and your hard-core drill music. And you, slightly unhealthy-looking man singing along to Robbie Williams duets. And you, social justice warrior rocking those chilled Lily Allen beats. And you, young student in your mother's car with the windows down and your funky shades trying to impress the laaaydeez. It doesn't matter who you are – on the motorway you can play your music as loud as you fucking want, but when you're driving through town stop acting like a prick and turn it down.

∼

Learn how to fucking park (part 3)

The final point for parking may sound like an obvious one, but FFS just park in the spaces where you're allowed to park. Don't park up on a double yellow line and stick your fucking hazard lights on, or pull over on the 'No waiting' zone because you're only dropping someone off. No waiting means no fucking waiting, not 'well you can wait for a bit so long as you don't turn your engine off'. While it might make your life infinitely easier, it will always be at the expense of making everyone else's life more difficult.

∼

Stay in your fucking lane

Zip merging (when two lanes are being merged into one) is one of the main hotspots for road rage, mainly because it conflicts with our own impeccable sense of queuing superiority. The law is to use both lanes until the point of merging, but some prefer to get in the correct lane as soon as possible, and go bumper to bumper with the car in front to prevent any queue jumpers barging in. It doesn't help that those who speed down to the front of the queue are generally those in a high performance Land Rover with overwhelming sense of smugness fitted as standard. What's not up for debate, however, is once you're in your lane, you stay in your fucking lane. A special place in hell is reserved for those who pull out, speed down the outside and then cut in again at the front.

∾

A lot of the rules laid out above are simply reminders of what we're taught when we learn to drive. The laws of the land that when broken are more than a social faux pas. But they're also the stuff we forget as the years go by. We get complacent and start to believe we're so good at driving that we can do other stuff as well, like eat a sandwich, or do our make-up, or make a film of us doing carpool karaoke like James Corden. And that's where the problems start. In fact, it's not just driving – many of the world's major issues start with James Corden.

The roads are there for us all to share, not for exclusive use by lorries or cars or bicycles or horses or Uber drivers or Deliveroo mopeds, and we've all got to get along. At the end of the day – and at the start – you have to accept that people will always drive like dicks, and you have to leave it to the authorities to sort them out at some point. It's not up to you to tell other people how to drive – but when other people's driving etiquette conflicts with our own, we feel obliged to tell them, with a horn, with a fist, with a finger, with a roll of the window and some colourful verbals. We need to resist the urge to switch into parent mode, so the next time a car (probably an Audi) forces their way smugly in front of you, show some fucking good manners and just smile and wave. It's better for everyone.

❧

4. THE CINEMA

∽

'The world is changed by your
example, not by your opinion.'
PAULO COELHO

∽

THE CINEMA

Manners at the cinema tend to attract more attention than many other public places, most likely because of the volume of people crammed into a small space, the increasing cost of tickets and the outrageous idea that people go there to actually watch a film. Not enjoy a meal. Not chat with friends or update their status. Not spend two hours sucking each other's faces off. No . . . you go to the cinema to watch a film. Unless it's a Michael Bay film, in which case you're probably fine to chat through most of it and just look at the pictures once in a while.

In 2010 the BBC's film critics Mark Kermode and Simon Mayo produced what many consider to be the Ten Commandments of film watching with their Cinema Code of Conduct, which covers off the major issues. Although their rule of not eating 'anything harder than a soft roll (with no filling)' is slightly limiting, especially when they have huge stalls selling overpriced popcorn outside. (While we're on the subject, the mark-up for most bags of popcorn is well above 1,000 per cent.) The basic rule is: sit down, shut up and watch the fucking film, but here are a few more specifics you might want to employ to make sure the fight scenes are all kept on the silver screen.

(Many of these apply to the theatre as well, but sporting events and music gigs are a different kettle of fish. If the general gist is to sit in silence, then do that; if some form of cheering, whooping or hollering is required, you can probably ignore most of what's below.)

∾

Don't be fucking late

Most cinema times are given for the start of the programme, before the adverts and trailers, so if it says 6.45pm, get there at 6.45pm. Give yourself time to buy whatever you need to, have a wee, find your correct seat and settle in for what you've paid your extortionate amount of money for. Five minutes late? Probably OK. Ten minutes? You'll miss the trailers, but anything after that and you should just go and watch something else. If you are so desperate to watch *Mamma Mia! Here We Go Again* for the fourth time and you're late, just take the nearest seat in the cinema that causes the least disruption to everyone else. It's your punishment for not being able to use a watch.

∾

Sit in your fucking seat

In direct contradiction to the last statement (which only applies if the film has already started) if you arrive on time (well done) then locate the seat that corresponds with the number on your ticket and make yourself comfy. Not the ones to the left a bit to avoid the tall man with big hair, or the VIP ones that you think no one's going to use anyway. There's a simple system cinemas employ to make sure everyone's sat in the correct seat and if one person ignores it, it screws it up for the rest of us. (Another notable exception to this rule is if your ticket sits you next to another person at an almost empty screening, which is a little creepy. It's unlikely the ticket office will do this, but use some common sense.)

~

Put your fucking feet down

Most cinemas now at least go some way to justifying their ridiculous prices by giving everyone plenty of leg space. But don't be fooled into thinking that gently resting your foot on the seat in front feels in any way gentle to the person sat there. Every tiny stretch or jolt is amplified to near-Jackie-Chan-strength proportions for them. In larger theatres, sneaking a foot through to the armrest is also unacceptable.

That's why it's called an armrest, not a footrest. And for the love of your deity of choice, keep your fucking shoes on.

✎

Turn your fucking phone off

Not on to vibrate. Not on to plane mode so you can play *Kim Kardashian: Hollywood* if you get bored. Off. Notable exceptions to this rule include: members of the emergency services, senior military figures with access to nuclear codes and people who have the ability to extract groups of school children from underground caves. Anyone else can most likely wait for the next two hours. If there's something else so demanding going on that it needs your immediate attention, then perhaps a night in with a DVD is the best course of action.

✎

Leave the kids at home

With some sort of trusted babysitter, obviously. Yes, this may instantly double the cost of your evening's entertainment but the basic rule is kids films are for kids, grown-up films are for grown-ups. There's an ever-expanding grey area around the age of twelve where adults are given the responsibility to decide if it's suitable or not. The answer to this lies in asking yourself if it's the film the kids would choose, or the film you want to see yourself. So don't drag little Primrose and Archie off to see *Life of Pi* in 3D on the big screen because you liked the book and think it'll teach them to appreciate the value of what they've got in life. It's about a boy scared shitless because he's stuck on a boat with an enormous fucking tiger. It'll have a similar effect on them too.

If your child is under the age of two then please do everyone – yourself included – a massive favour and go to the baby screenings. No one's under the delusion that everyone will sit in perfect silence throughout, and there's always someone on hand with extra wipes if there's an involuntary 'spillage' after feeding.

~

Keep your fucking head down

Yes, tall people must be allowed to go to the cinema, and most theatres are now staggered well enough that this rarely causes a problem. However, if you are lucky enough to be over six foot, or you share hairstyles with Jedward or ex-Nottingham Forest striker Jason Lee, or you're just really fond of large hats, then please do your best not to sit at full height.

If you do find yourself with someone impeding your view, you could try politely asking them to sit lower down, but this can be taken as an assault on their vertical superiority or coiffurial inferiority. Perhaps best to ask the staff if you can be moved.

❧

Get a fucking room

Not a seat in the back of the cinema: a room in a hotel or youth hostel or your mate's house while his parents are away. Or go to the park, or a bus shelter, or somewhere where your over-ambitious PDAs are less likely to cause people sat nearby to vomit uncontrollably. I understand the temptation of a darkened room for young romantics to use it as a time to get to know each other in the back rows, but your heightened enjoyment is directly proportional to other people's suffering. You're here to watch the fucking film – feel free to hold hands, have a little peck or even a squeeze of a knee. But FFS leave it at that.

❧

Leave it clean and fucking tidy

There are sometimes polite and often underpaid staff whose job it is to make sure the cinema is clean before the next screening, but you can make everything run a whole lot smoother by carrying your empty drinks and trays to the bin at the door. You're going that way anyway. In the event of a huge spillage resist the temptation to smash it into the floor with your foot and clear up what you can at the end of the film.

～

Keep it fucking quiet (part 1)

We're here to watch the film. And listen to it, too. Things we're not here to listen to include, but are not limited to: your views on the storyline and where it will end up; how you would have shot a particular scene; why this is typical of Wes Anderson's work; any continuity errors or flaws in the plot; what you think is about to happen; how this is a bit different from the book; any knowledge about the actor's/actress's sexual preferences; what kind of food you'd like afterwards. Just about all necessary communication required in the cinema ('Can you pass the popcorn?', 'Can I have a drink?') can be achieved through the medium of sign language.

～

Keep it fucking quiet (part 2)

On a similar note, please ensure when exiting the auditorium that all conversations including spoilers to what you've just seen are put on hold until you're out of earshot of everyone waiting to go in. Or at the very least not broadcast at full volume across the foyer.

∽

Keep it fucking quiet (part 3)

Perhaps the greatest debate on cinema etiquette revolves around food and drink. The idea of not eating 'anything harder than a soft roll (with no filling)' is a little overkill, and you have to stick to what's sold in the concession stalls. But there are ways of eating and drinking that make the whole experience fairly tolerable to others around you: don't delve into the depths of your popcorn or pic 'n' mix as if you're a six year old trying to extract a plastic toy from a cereal box; don't try and fit a whole fistful into your mouth at once; don't slurp around the bottom of your drink like you did when you were five; and don't buy any food that needs to be individually unwrapped before eating it. Granddad's Werther's Originals will just have to stay at home.

❧

Go to the fucking toilet before the start

Just like you would before setting off on a long journey. Many films break the two-hour mark these days, and there's a possibility you've just drunk a bin-sized vessel of soft drink, but having a quick wee beforehand will help. If you do have to go, then do make sure you avoid asking your fellow cinema-goers to fill you in on what you missed, when you return.

A year or two ago someone created an app called RunPee; a clever thing that told you when the best time to use the toilet was in any film without missing too much. Of course this overlooks the fact that no one should be using a fucking mobile phone in the first place, which renders it fairly pointless.

❧

No trip to the cinema is ever going to be completely perfect – we're all guilty of breaking a few of these rules from time to time. But we can at least do our best to consider those around us so we can all enjoy the film. Unless it's been directed by Lars Von Trier, in which case 'enjoy' is probably the wrong word.

❧

5. THE SHOPS

❧

'People buy things they don't need, with money they don't have, to impress people they don't like.'
CLIVE HAMILTON, *GROWTH FETISH*[11]

❧

THE SHOPS

Surprise and unsubstantiated fact of the day!: no one enjoys supermarket shopping. Even the people who say they do are only saying that to be smug about it. People can tolerate it at best, but no one takes genuine pleasure from it. There's simply too much to complain about: if it's not the food, it's the prices; if it's not the staff, it's the other customers; if it's not the quality of deconstructed doughnuts, it's the lack of organic kimchi.

And away from the supermarket aisles the experience isn't that much more enjoyable. Overpriced car parks; endless queues; lack of stock; walking for miles; obnoxious store assistants; over-enthusiastic store assistants; under-enthusiastic store assistants, and, let's not forget the biggest pain of all – other shoppers. How fucking dare they come and shop on the same day? How dare they spend more than a fraction of a second deciding if something would go well with their imitation leather trousers? How dare they apply for a store card at the checkout when everyone knows that the only thing you should do at the till is Pay. For. Your. Fucking. Goods.

In recent years the whole hellish shopping nightmare has been pushed to extremes by the introduction of Black Friday. I'm sure we've all seen the pictures and read the stories about the global lunacy that surrounds this frenzied day of mass consumerism. As George Monbiot wrote in *The Guardian*:

> '[Governments] regard it as a sacred duty to encourage the country's most revolting spectacle: the annual feeding frenzy in which shoppers queue all night, then stampede into the shops, elbow, trample and sometimes fight to be the first to carry off some designer junk which will go into landfill before the sales next year. The madder the orgy, the greater the triumph of economic management.'[12]

There's even a website – the candidly-named www.blackfridaydeathcount.com – set up to record the number of injuries (and sadly deaths) that have occurred on this day in recent years. All in the name of saving a few quid on a TV that will most likely be out of date in a couple of years, or a pair of trainers that will only ever be seen on someone's Instagram account. A few of the lowlights include:

> 2016 – Shirtless man uses belt as a whip outside Vancouver Black Friday sale
> 2016 – Huge Black Friday riot breaks out over discounted TOILET ROLLS

2018 – 'They are like animals': Nutella
sale sparks Black Friday-style riots at
supermarkets throughout France

2018 – Angry shoppers square off in pre-Black
Friday scuffle at Palmdale Walmart,
California[13]

A very fucking Black Friday, indeed. But perhaps
equally bizarre was the online outrage in 2018 when
people failed to display Armageddon-style looting
behaviour, with many businesses and shoppers
deciding to stay well clear of the high street shenanigans and shop online instead. As *The Guardian*
reported on 23 November:

> '"Pls entertain me": shortage of Black Friday
> brawls prompts online gripes.'[14]

The problem with shopping is that everyone needs
what's on offer (or, more likely, just wants it), but no
one can really be bothered to invest the time it takes
to do it properly. Over the years we've been lulled
into a sense of entitlement that means we expect
everything to be available wherever and whenever
we want it. ('What do you mean you don't have
any dried barberries? I need it for my Ottolenghi
recipe.')

But while trendy marketing departments all over the world are busy brain-storming/thought-showering/ideating over how to amplify our in-store brand experiences with crèches and coffee points and lighting systems designed to turn us into consumerist zombies, some simple fucking good manners would probably be the best place to start.

❧

Learn how to push a fucking trolley

At the time of writing, there's no requirement in the UK – or any part of the world to my knowledge – to have a licence to push a supermarket trolley. There's no written exam or driving test you need to pass, there's no speed limit to stick to and the aisles aren't covered in road markings, stop signs and traffic lights. As far as I can see that's for two main reasons:

1) Severe injury or death is unlikely to result from a collision of supermarket trolleys. (Although in 2013 a woman was arrested for manslaughter when an elderly man died after being hit by her shopping trolley. In M&S of all places.)

2) It's up to people to use their common sense, and indeed their manners, to push the fucking things.

So please, try and show some decency towards others while pushing your trolley – maintain a sensible speed, slow down at junctions, let people through with a cheery smile (that's unlikely to be reciprocated) and avoid spinning doughnuts in the aisles. Should the odd accidental collision occur then don't lose your shit and start screaming at people. A friendly smile is fine.

∾

Learn how to park a fucking trolley

Equally important is how to leave your fucking trolley if you just need to nip down an aisle to grab something. Don't leave it in the middle of the aisle or next to something popular where it's likely to get in the way. Push it over to one side and out of the way. On your return, if someone's reaching across to try and grab something, do your best impersonation of a human by holding your hands up and saying the words 'Sorry – let me just get that out of the way for you'. Conversely, if you find someone's trolley abandoned in front of your organic granola, then avoid the temptation to send it flying across the aisle and bitch at the person when they return. Instead, gently push it to one side and retrieve what you need.

❧

Cut the fucking chit-chat

Supermarkets are for shopping. Bars, cafés, restaurants, benches, parks and long coastal walks are good places to chat with friends. Of course you may well bump into an old colleague, and these serendipitous moments are delightful. But once you've switched from grocery-shopping mode into chit-chat mode then please do so in a place that allows everyone else to continue with their primary task of shopping. That might be at the end of the aisle, or next to the gluten-free shampoo, but do make sure that you're not stood side by side in the middle of the fucking aisle blocking everyone else from getting past.

❧

Keep dithering to a minimum

The numbers vary depending on which report you read, but UK supermarkets have been known to stock anything up to 90,000 products. Tesco was generally considered to be the worst offender, at one point stocking 224 varieties of air freshener, 98 types of rice, 60 varieties of Cola and a mind-boggling 283 options for coffee. Most weekly shops consist of about 100 items (or 0.25 per cent of the store), so a little dawdling is forgivable. But in the interests of everyone getting along, do just have a look around you as you scrutinise the ingredients for fifteen minutes. Have a glance over your shoulder and if someone looks like they might need something you're blocking, then get out of the fucking way.

∾

Put your fucking phone away

There are many perfectly good reasons to have your phone out as you go around the supermarket. In fact, quite often a chat with your bezzie about last night's shenanigans while browsing the aisles can be quite useful, if your multitasking skills are up to scratch. Sadly few people's are. So let's make this as clear as possible: if you're on the phone – whether it's talking, texting, sexting, listening to music or podcasts or playing *Farmville* – you're not fucking ready to check out. Turn it off, hang up, take your headphones out and enjoy a proper human-to-human interaction that shows some respect for the person who's paid a fairly crappy wage to help you purchase your blinis for tonight's canapés.

❧

Get your fucking money/coupons ready

It shouldn't come as a great surprise that job number one when paying for your groceries, is to pay for your fucking groceries. You can make this much easier for everyone by doing it as quickly as possible and having everything ready once it's all been scanned. There's never any fucking need to extend your conversation with the cashier past the usual formalities.

If you do find yourself in a situation where you've forgotten your wallet, or left the coupons in the car, or your card's been frozen by a bitter ex-partner, then show a little fucking humility and offer some form of verbal apology to everyone behind you. At the very minimum you should adopt a facial expression that shows some sort of remorse, rather than standing there all hoity-toity-like and blaming the cashier for holding everyone up.

❧

Put your fucking trolley back

You'll notice there are people in most supermarket car parks whose job it is to return trolleys to the front of the store for new customers to use. Please don't take this as a challenge to make them earn their wage by dumping your trolley in the nearest empty space or bush. You have it in your power to help these highly underpaid people do their job even more efficiently by taking ten to fifteen seconds to return your trolley to the nearest trolley park. Be that person – for extra superhero status you could even consider removing any old lists or wrappers from the bottom of it.

❧

Learn how to stand in a fucking line
See Chapter 7.

❧

Put it back where it fucking came from
If you decide you no longer need an item, then put it back where you fucking got it from. Or send the kids to do it if that's too much hassle, or give it to a store assistant, or even the cashier. But please don't put a tray of raw prawns back on the fucking dried pasta shelf because you can't be bothered to go back.

❧

Help people reach stuff
It'll fill you momentarily with a warm, fuzzy feeling. Enjoy it while it lasts.

❧

Next fucking customer, please

You've successfully loaded up the belt with your weekly shop, arranging items in a way that makes maximum use of the space, and helps to bag them in an orderly manner at the other end. Nice work. But failure to put the divider in place afterwards can cause all manner of anxiety issues for some, so please pop the fucking thing down so the next person can start loading up their items.

❧

Learn how to use
a fucking cash machine

Insert card, enter pin, select amount, take card, take cash, next person, please. That's as long as your transaction should take. Banks don't help the process by adding a host of 'useful' features such as topping up your mobile, paying in cheques, paying bills, transferring money, buying stamps, and donating to charity. Cash machines are for getting some fucking cash. If you need to do anything else then go inside and speak to someone about it.

❧

Be careful with your fucking umbrella

While navigating between shops in the rain, please display some simple umbrella etiquette by adjusting its height so you don't smack someone in the fucking face with it. It can be tricky, yes, but make some fucking effort instead of lowering it down over your eyes and barging through.

～

Don't use your pram as a fucking battering ram

Naturally, if you're out shopping with your new-born, then people should make a bit more of an effort to get out of your way. But that doesn't entitle you to fucking hurtle towards people at high-speed and then stare at them like they've bitch-slapped your child when they nearly bump into you. If there are two or more pushchairs in your group then it's your responsibility to make space for other people by temporarily suspending your essential conversation about reflux, and forming a single line, instead of taking up the whole fucking pavement.

～

As you can tell, most manners in the retail world revolve around an appreciation that you've come to the shops to shop, and anything above that isn't entirely fucking necessary. Stores do their best to give you pointers on how to behave, and most now understand the importance of making the whole experience as tolerable as possible for you, with wider aisles, simpler choices and more people on the checkout tills. But that isn't always the case. It's down to us to help each other out, treat everyone with a bit of respect and stop focusing on what's easiest for ourselves.

Lower your expectations of what you'll achieve, raise your understanding that it might not be all that fun, and the chances are that you'll find the whole fucking experience a lot more satisfying.

~

6. PUBLIC TOILETS

❧

'The flush toilet, more than any single invention, has "civilized" us in a way that religion and law could never accomplish.'

THOMAS LYNCH, *THE UNDERTAKING: LIFE STUDIES FROM THE DISMAL TRADE*[15]

❧

PUBLIC TOILETS

Toilets, lavatories, restrooms, washrooms, loos, WCs, latrines, bogs, throne rooms, shitters, dunnies, khazies, heads, privies, crappers. Whatever you call them, they can be pretty dirty places. Literally, and often figuratively too. They are also one of the few (legal) places on the planet where our private lives and personal hygiene standards are publicly held up against other people's, so our behaviour comes under closer scrutiny than in most other places. Some people like them to be clean enough to perform open-heart surgery in there, others seem happy to leave their own piss all over the toilet seat and wipe any residue off on their trousers on the way out. (Because . . . obviously if you can't feel or see any germs on your hands, then there aren't any.) What we should remember is that we've all most likely experienced that desperate, buttock-clenched dash into a cubicle where you would happily sell your child's soul for a clean, sparkly seat in front of you. You can be the unknown hero who makes that possible. Take some pride in that.

Generally, public toilets and restrooms around the world are seeing hugely improved standards of sanitation, and many are monitored on an hourly basis. Some even have those little smiley/sad face buttons that you can push on your way out to express your satisfaction or extreme anger. Problems normally occur when alcohol or drugs are involved, impairing our judgement, as well as our aim. Hence, there are no rules in this section that apply to festival toilets. My only advice there, is to make sure you have your own toilet paper and enough hand sanitiser to clean an elephant.

The Brits in particular seem to be infamous for their obsession with toilets. Just as Eskimos have more than 50 words for snow, the British have over 200 words for the act of defecation. But despite all the talk of wee and poo and farts and stuff, we have to remain fairly grown-up about the subject, because failure to comply with the rules of toilet etiquette can result in all manner of awkward situations.

∼

Keep your fucking distance

Gentlemen – you know the rule, even if you've never said it out loud. If there's an option to leave a space between you and your fellow urinater, then do so. If you have the choice of three empty urinals, choose either of the outside ones, allowing room for someone else to use the other without standing next to you.

If you're at a trough that has no partitions, then leave a good six inches between elbows so there's no accidental body contact. Don't be the twat (usually at sporting venues) who sees a small gap and chirps up with a cheery 'Make room for one more'. Once a person is in place, they should never be asked to move.

~

Zip it

Mouths as well as trouser flies. A brief acknowledgement is acceptable, but no more than that. Once you're in full flow then don't engage in any sort of conversation, no matter how essential. Away from the urinals – while washing your hands, for example – is OK for basic chat, excluding religion, politics and Piers Morgan. Never hold conversations between closed cubicles.

Ladies, having little first-hand knowledge of toilet banter in the female washroom, and without wishing to reinforce stereotypes, I believe the rules on conversation are a little more relaxed. But bear in mind that everyone can hear what you're saying, so don't engage in anything too heavy.

☙

Keep your eyes to the front

There's no need to turn your head to either side while at the urinal. Up and down is fine, but not repeatedly or too rapidly. You'll just have to make do with reading the advert for incontinence pants or the police recruitment campaign.

☙

Wait for the hand dryer

Not so much a rule for etiquette, just a handy hint for those worried about making a bit too much noise while 'dropping the kids off at the pool'. Waiting for a bit of background noise to cover up any aggressive movements can prevent awkward situations upon leaving the stalls and bumping into your boss.

☙

Use your fucking hands

There's an increasing trend – for want of a better word – for people to use their foot to flush the toilet or open the automatic doors on train cubicles. This may help you avoid the risk of touching anything mucky with your hand, but it means that everyone else after you has to put up with a shitty button. And while no one is likely to witness this act (therefore avoiding what some would consider bad manners) it doesn't stop it from being really fucking antisocial. If you're really fussed then use a piece of paper to push the flush or use your elbow to push the door button, but washing your fucking hands properly should solve most issues.

❧

Lift the fucking seat up

Seriously, if you've got through life to the age where you can read without learning to lift the seat up when you pee (gents, not ladies), then you should really have a deep and meaningful conversation with your parents. Or at least a strongly-worded text message. Most people do this out of habit at home, so it shouldn't be any different in public. Use a couple of sheets of toilet paper for protection if it's in a bit of a state, but don't use it as an excuse to cover it in even more piss. And don't forget to put the fucking thing back down again once you're done.

❧

Put your fucking phone away

There was a time when using a mobile phone in a public toilet was just seen as a bit weird and gross.

That was in the days before every phone had a twelve-megapixel, wide-angle, telephoto lens with optical image stabilisation built in to it. Now using your phone in a toilet is weird, gross and more than a touch creepy as well. You may well feel comfortable updating your Facebook status or playing *Where's My Water?* at home, but phones should stay in pockets once you've stepped through the doors. Find some other place for the #toilets #handswashed #ready selfie.

෨

Wait your fucking turn

There is no hierarchy in the world of public toilets. It makes no difference who you are, how much you earn, or who once liked one of your tweets. It's first come, first served. If it's verging on a matter of life or death, then you have a responsibility to apologise to everyone in front of you, beg their forgiveness and offer to buy them a drink.

෨

Don't gob your fucking gum in the urinal

You've been chewing on a piece of spearmint Orbit for so long it feels like a dog toy. And probably tastes like one too. You're answering the call of nature and the opportunity to dispose of your gum presents itself in front of you. Please resist this urge. Not only because there's probably a bin about five feet behind you, but because some poor doofus has the job of removing that piece of piss-riddled gum.

∾

Get some help

Possibly the most awkward situation a fully-grown human can be faced with is a blocked toilet. Whether you did the damage or not, you discovered it, so you have a responsibility to do something about it. Go outside, find someone, tell them it was like that already if you want. Just be grateful that you don't have to fix it yourself and remember that you'll probably never see that person again.

∾

Keep it clean

The golden rule of toiletness. As an adult, a human, a halfway-intelligent member of society, your minimum responsibility to the toilet world is to leave them as you found them. Clear up after yourself, wash your hands and make sure the only thing you leave behind is an olfactory eyebrow-raiser. Some prefer a 'leave it as you'd like to find it' rule, which is highly considerate, but largely unrealistic unless you happen to carry a mop, bucket and a tin of paint around with you.

(If you are on the more obsessive end of the hygiene spectrum and worry about ending up in something that resembles a scene from Trainspotting, *I can highly recommend the app Flush, which gives you locations, directions and – most importantly – ratings for public toilets near you, all around the world. Just remember to put your phone away once you find it.)*

❧

As mentioned at the start, the difficulty with toilet etiquette is that different people have different standards – both of hygiene and personal awareness. You can put up as many humorous signs as you want about not sprinkling when you're tinkling, but it's not going to matter to some coked-up muppet who's just had a dodgy kebab. The truth is the only thing that genuinely matters is that all the dirty stuff goes where the dirty stuff belongs. The manners are all optional extras – you can chat on your phone, take selfies, start conversations with strangers, bang on the doors or push to the front of the queue and no one's going to arrest you. But the point is not about behaving in a manner we're comfortable with, it's about behaving in a way that makes everyone else feel comfortable. And in public toilets that's more difficult than anywhere else.

∾

7. QUEUING

❧

'Manners require time, and nothing
is more vulgar than haste.'
RALPH WALDO EMERSON

❧

QUEUING

For something that's essentially standing in a line, queues are a lot more fucking complicated than you might think. Different types of queue have different rules and behaviour that people will or won't tolerate. Whether you're waiting at midnight to buy the latest Harry Potter book, online to buy tickets to the Spice Girls reunion tour, waiting to ride the teacups at Disneyland or for Bros to sign an intimate part of your body, queuing correctly is an essential part of modern etiquette. Especially if you're a Brit.

Why the British are held up as such a prime example of queuing correctness is a bit of a mystery. Yes, there are some outstanding examples of the Brits' obsession with queues – such as the annual queue at Wimbledon – but it's more likely that we just enjoy the opportunity to prove our civility and moral superiority. But take a look at the scrum that precedes a Ryanair flight to Malaga, or the chaos surrounding a Wetherspoon's bar on a Friday evening – the Brits can be just as selfish and twatish as any other nation.

The Brits' obsession with queuing dates back to the Industrial Revolution, but it was the Second World War, when the country desperately needed some order among all the pandemonium around them, that really made the country pull its figurative socks up. Rationing began in early 1940 when citizens were asked to calmly wait in line to receive their allowance of essentials, and, with all the fighting going on across Europe, it made little sense to start another scrap over some bacon and eggs. Some fucking order was needed, as was a sense of community and fairness, so people did their duty. No doubt this ability to 'keep your head when all about you, are losing theirs and blaming it on you',[16] gave great pride to many and established the British as completely unofficial and self-proclaimed world champions of queuing. (International cricket had been cancelled during the war, so we had to make something up that we were good at.)

The Wimbledon queue is now held up as an example of our quirky love of queuing, with thousands camping out for days to get their chance to see a couple of people hitting a yellow ball backwards and forwards across a net. It even has its own Code of Conduct with thirteen rules to be followed, including no bagsying places, no toilet breaks longer than 30 minutes, no barbecues or camping stoves and no ball games after 10pm. But pop over the Atlantic and even Wimbledon pales in comparison to

Duke University's official queuing policy for their basketball games, which weighs in at an impressively persnickety 36 pages. The truth is probably less that the British enjoy standing in a fucking queue, and more that we admire the sense of order and decorum that can be found in an otherwise chaotic situation.

According to a TripAdvisor report in 2017, here are the top ten worst tourist queues (or best, depending on how you like to spend your time).

1. London Eye: two-and-a-half hours (skip the line for £32.45)
2. Sistine Chapel and Vatican: two hours (priority access £28)
3. Colosseum, Rome: two hours (priority access £41)
4. Catacombs, Paris: two hours, up to three–four hours during summer (priority access tour £28)
5. Eiffel Tower, Paris: two hours (priority access £15)
6. St Peter's Basilica, Vatican City: one-and-a-half hours (priority access £17)
7. Tower of London: one-and-a-half hours (tour access £30)

8. Van Gogh Museum, Amsterdam: one-and-a-half hours (guided tour £80)

9. Empire State Building, New York: one-and-a-half hours (tour access £60)

10. Notre-Dame Cathedral, Paris: one hour (tour access £28)*[17]

Wherever you are in the world, the idea of first come, first served is one that should resonate with most people, whether you're queuing in a grocery store, at a bar or on a motorway. (Sadly there's not much anyone can do about telephone queues, made all the more annoying when you're routinely cut off after 45 minutes listening to messages saying how important your call is to them.) Orderly queuing shows some fucking respect for those around you and an appreciation of other people's needs, whether you're leaving your shoes in line in Thailand, or marking your place with some sticky tape in Japan. Here are a few other pointers to make sure you don't step out of line when you're stood in line.

༄

---

* Now closed for a spot of refurbishment.

Use your fucking ears

Planes have a helpful system to allow passengers to board the plane in the quickest possible time. It goes like this: they call out the rows that should board first; they let them get on, shove their bags in the lockers and take a seat; they let the next group on. It's not that fucking difficult. Listen carefully, check your ticket and board when they ask you to, not when your ingrained sense of entitlement tells you to.

⮑

Don't double lane

A popular method often practised by families and groups queuing for airport check-in desks is to split the party to see which queue will go faster. Once one party nears the front, the other party moves across. Any brief feelings of joy experienced by the people in the queue that is now shorter, is completely offset by the despair, frustration and seething hatred of the people who now have a group of twenty queuing in front of them. Most airports use a single 'serpentine' line to prevent this kind of behaviour, and it makes sure we're all equally unhappy shuffling our bags along and nervously checking our watches.

❧

Know your fucking place

The queue for the bar has no such order, so it's up to the customers to demonstrate some civility to each other and notify the barman of the correct order that people should be served in. Sadly, all too often it's the pissed-up muppet who shouts the loudest who gets served first. Don't be this person. You're better than that. Just like in the hairdressers, take a note of who's standing there when you arrive, and wait for them to be served before ordering your eighteen fucking cocktails.

❧

Pay attention

If you're waiting at the bar, then wait at the fucking bar. If you're chatting with your mates, reading the *Racing Post* or checking your fucking acca on your mobile phone, then you are not waiting at the fucking bar. If the bar's busy then move away once you've got your drinks so there's space for everyone else.

❧

Don't fucking cut in

When a cashier opens a new checkout in the super-market or other large stores, the first person they serve should be the first person in the nearest queue who hasn't already started to load their groceries onto the belt. In reality, it's usually the person at the very back of the queue who just happened to be paying attention when the cashier returned from their cigarette break. If that person happens to be you, then pause for half a second, offer it to the person in front of you, and take some pleasure from the fact that people aren't secretly wishing bad things happen to you.

❧

Leave some fucking personal space

As desperate as you may be to get to the front of the line, leading scientists have discovered pushing as close to the person in front of you as possible makes fuck-all difference to the speed you'll be served. In long queues a gap of six inches is fine, in shorter queues you can give them a bit more personal space. Equally, don't leave a massive gap – keep the queue moving and people tend to be a bit less miserable.

❧

Keep your kids entertained

Most grown-ups can get their heads around the concept that queues are a necessary pain for the pleasure that lies at the end – be it a holiday, a cinnamon soy latte or a chat with your mortgage adviser. Kids, however, are yet to learn this, and need a few things to occupy their minds. Give them a book, a tablet, a roll of Sellotape – whatever it fucking takes to keep them happy. Happy kids = happy you = happy (ish) queue.

ᔑ

Stay in the fucking line

Unless you've formed some sort of verbal agreement with the people behind you, or there are rules that permit you to do otherwise, once you're in the queue, you stay in the fucking queue. There's always a bit of flexibility – a couple of steps to grab some chewing gum is fine – but once you've physically left the queue, you start again at the back. No excuses. No leaving your trolley in line to fetch the organic arugula you forgot. The back.

ᔑ

Get yourself fucking ready

After waiting 37 minutes at airport security for someone to scan your personal belongings and check you're not carrying a lethal cocktail of 200 millilitres of mineral water, it shouldn't come as a surprise when you finally reach the front. You can make sure this time isn't wasted by taking the coins out of your pockets, undoing your belt and shoes, removing your watch and taking out whatever intimate piercings you've decided make you a more interesting person. So when you get to the front you're actually fucking ready to go through.

Once you've been cleared of any potential terrorist threat, don't just stand there in the middle of everyone, exposing your girth to the world as you put your belt back on. Grab your belongings and move to the side so you're not blocking the fucking way for everyone else.

～

Be nice at the front

However long you've been waiting in your designated queue, however desperate you've been, however important it is you catch that train, be fucking nice to the person who serves you at the front. It's rarely their fault, and having a childish meltdown because you're going to be late won't speed anything up. Plus there are equally desperate people behind you, who just want you to shut the fuck up and get out of the way. Deep breath, big smile and get on with buying your vegan sausage roll.

~

Get off your fucking phone

Yes, phones again. While they're a great way to occupy yourself when standing in the line, they should be nowhere to be seen when you reach the front. Your job description has changed from 'wait patiently' to 'get out of here as quickly as fucking possible', so anything that inhibits your ability to achieve this should be removed. Plus it shows a real lack of respect for the person serving you.

~

Bus queues

Much like queues at bars and pubs, the bus queue is often left for people to manage themselves, and the resulting scrum can result in weapons-grade tutting and teeth sucking. We're left to police the situation for ourselves, so as fine, outstanding citizens with a sense of pride and respect for others, it's up to us to take a look at who was there first and let them on first. Yes, some possibly young and probably headphone-wearing toe-rag will take advantage of your kindness, but they'll learn one day. Or perhaps they won't but, look . . . just leave it.

❧

The important thing for all queues is an equal sense of fairness, whether it's completely fair for everyone, or completely unfair. The problems arise when someone discovers a loophole for the queue and people feel their good nature is being taken advantage of, or someone is getting one over on them. Anyone who's waited patiently to go on the Peter Pan ride at Disneyland will know the sense of outrageous injustice when some smug family waltzes up to the front of the queue with their FASTPASS. We're all short of time and stressed about getting home and desperate to let Timmy meet Hagrid's body double (ex-England second row Martin Bayfield, btw). But as soon as we assume our needs are more important than someone else's, then everything descends into utter fucking chaos.

❧

8. NEIGHBOURS AND COMMUNITY

∾

*'There are two things we wish we could live
without: haemorrhoids and neighbours.'*

SPIKE MILLIGAN

∾

NEIGHBOURS AND COMMUNITY

As a child of the late eighties and early nineties, it's difficult to say the word neighbours without following it immediately with 'everybody needs good neighbours' and conjuring a mental image of Todd Landers skidding into screen on his BMX. *Neighbours* – Australia's longest-running soap opera – gave many of us our first insight into the eclectic mix and complexities of a small community in Erinsborough, teaching us many essential life lessons along the way, including:

- Incorrect protestor protocol when taking part in an anti-duck hunting rally.
- How to survive being kidnapped by an Ecuadorian drug cartel.
- The dangers of kissing your wife while driving along a narrow coastal road on your wedding day.
- How to deal with finding pictures of your sister in a porno.
- What dogs dream about.
- How to perform an emergency tracheotomy during a tornado.

- How to reintegrate yourself into society five years after you were supposedly washed out to sea.
- What to do when your towel gets jammed in the front door and you're left naked on the street.
- The damaging ramifications of accusing your Chinese neighbours of eating your dog.

Above all, *Neighbours* taught us all how to forgive those in our local community when they inevitably try to strangle us, run off with our loved ones, steal our life savings, or spy on us having sex to use as inspiration for a new career as a romance novelist. *That's* when good neighbours become good friends.

But real life can almost be as scary as fiction, and comes complete with its own soap operas that put the antics of Ramsay Street's residents in the shade. Our tabloid newspapers are full of stories about feuding neighbours, whether it's an angry dispute over the height of fences, bitter objections over nude sunbathing, or eviction notices being served for making too much noise while having sex. Many of these conflicts are the result of months and years of minor disagreements building up, until one last straw finally breaks the camel's back. And once that back's broken, it's very fucking difficult to fix again.

What begins as an innocent failure to return a *Little Britain* box set (that you never really wanted back) is flamed by some fucking selfish parking, then starts to take hold when you witness their cat shitting in your flower bed, and finally blazes out of control when they drunkenly start singing 'I Think We're Alone Now' at two in the morning. No matter how much these petty acts may leave you pacing your hallway and twitching your curtains, you're better off having your neighbours on your side. Not just in case you run out of sugar, or need to borrow a pressure washer, but because they're the closest living human being to your home. Saying Hi on the odd occasion, sending a couple of Christmas cards and chucking back a football every now and again is a relatively small price to pay to someone who could potentially save you from burning to death, or provide shelter when the world starts committing mass suicide because they've seen some really weird and fucked up monster.

There's an old maxim you've probably heard that 'An Englishman's home is his castle'. Aside from the obvious issues with gender inequality, this adage is generally trotted out by people who believe they have the right to do whatever the fuck they like inside their boundary walls. Yes – everyone's home should be a place where they feel protected (e.g. a castle), but if we're going to elevate our homes to castle status, then we should also raise our levels of duty and responsibility to equally regal levels. You can't have Castle Grayskull without the responsibility to prance around in a furry jockstrap protecting the realm from the evil forces of Skeletor.

It's not easy. We can't make everyone see eye-to-eye. We can't live in some twee utopia where everyone has glorious smiles and bakes cookies for each other all day. But we can do our best to demonstrate an awareness of those outside our castle walls and show them some fucking decency (regardless of whether they necessarily deserve it or not). The police have got far more important things to deal with than a fight that broke out over four inches of garden fence.

Other than the price of homes there's nothing that really dictates who should live where, so we're all jammed in together – old people living next to young, drag queens next to burger kings, aspiring hip-hop artists next to alcoholic estate agents, cat-loving Brexiteers next to dog-loving Remoaners. People from all walks of life rubbing up against each other, which is why demonstrating some fucking good manners is essential to keep everything running smoothly.

∾

Say hello

That's pretty much all it takes. A simple hello, followed by a generic formal introduction, involving the exchange of names and where you live – if it isn't already blindingly obvious. Give them a wave and a smile every now and again, and if you get the chance to progress onto more erudite conversation at a later date then count it as a bonus, but keep it simple. Similarly, if you see someone moving in then go and say hello. Joining the book club, neighbourhood watch association and residents' swingers club can all come at a later date.

∾

Keep the fucking noise down (part 1)

Noise is probably the biggest source of neighbourly disputes. Whether it's from a late night party, some early morning DIY, an insecure dog or an overly enthusiastic display of love-making, excess noise deprives people of one of their most treasured things – sleep. On the other hand, while sleep does rank a little higher as a basic human necessity than singing Bonnie Tyler or doing some topiary, that shouldn't dictate you have to be tiptoeing around for all hours of the day or night. Get some headphones, some nice comfy slippers, some intensive psychological therapy for your dog or whatever it takes to create a bit of fucking harmony. It's better for everyone.

∽

Show some fucking respect

Love – in the biblical sense of the word, or otherwise – is a strong word to describe how you should feel towards your neighbours. In an ideal world then yes, love's the benchmark we should be aiming for, but in reality we should probably move through the gears of 'not hating' and 'just about tolerating' before we start patting ourselves on the back. So stop sticking your fucking nose into everything that they do and being such a fucking NIMBY.

∽

Keep it clean and fucking tidy

It doesn't have to be perfect striped lawns and rosebushes, but if your front garden/yard looks like the aftermath of the Fyre Festival then prepare yourself for some passive-aggressive notes through your letterbox. Show a little consideration for your neighbours and keep it clean. Put your rubbish where it fucking belongs – if you don't have space for it in your bins, then find another (legal) way to dispose of it.

~

Take some fucking responsibility

No matter how much you cherish your adorable children or your gorgeous Rottweiler that's just-a-big-baby-and-would-never-hurt-a-soul, you have to understand that to some people they're a pain in the fucking arse. It's perfectly possible that your neighbours' only knowledge of their existence is seeing them shit on the pavement (the pets, not the children) or loitering at the bus stop in their hoodies. If you have either children or pets, you have to accept that they are your fucking responsibility, and you are accountable for their actions.

~

Pick their shit up

Dog mess – or shit as it's more frequently known by those who've stepped in the stuff – is fucking gross. This is so blatantly obvious that I feel slightly stupid having to even write the words down. It's actual poo. With actual fucking shit germs in it. That can cause people to go actually fucking blind. But it's not obvious, because people still leave the stuff lying

113

around all over the place. Bag that shit up and put it in the fucking bin – not the hedge or hanging from a fucking branch.

∾

Keep the fucking noise down (part 2)

Many etiquette books have a neighbourhood party as a good means of building bridges with neighbours and demonstrating your willingness to integrate with the community. And that's just tickety-boo if you live in a nice leafy street where everyone has glorious smiles that hide so many sordid secrets. If you're having a party, just accept that everyone outside the party is hating it as much as everyone inside is enjoying it – show some consideration and know when enough is fucking enough.

∾

Don't park like a twat

It'd be great if we could all park directly outside our front doors, but the reality is that the number of cars, combined with the ever-increasing size of them, means this rarely happens. Even if people do have driveways, garages, car parks or on-street spaces, any system can be thrown into chaos by an influx of guests or new vehicles, so essentially it's left up to us all to park with a bit of common-fucking-sense. If you're blocking a driveway or garage (including failing to give enough space to actually turn in and out of it), or parking on a junction, or getting in the way of traffic or filling the street with five cars because your kids have moved back home, then you are not parking with a bit of common-fucking-sense.

~

Stop leaving fucking passive-aggressive notes

If you wouldn't say it to someone's face, then don't stick it on a piece of paper on the front door or windscreen. Of course it's easier and there's less chance of them trying to put your head through the fucking wall, but anonymous notes in real life serve no more purpose than an anonymous comment online. Either leave it alone or go and talk to them.

~

Don't take the fucking piss

'Neither a borrower nor a lender be; For loan oft loses both itself and friend.' Polonius – from William Shakespeare's *Hamlet* – has a point, but he'd make a bit of a prick for a neighbour.

Whether it's the BBC's official DVD of Harry and Meghan's wedding (complete with exclusive unseen footage and bonus features), a hand blender or the dining room table, what you borrow needs to be fucking returned in as good a state as when they lent it to you, if not better. Should you find yourself constantly borrowing things from your neighbours, without ever returning the favour, then entertain the possibility that you're becoming a pain in the fucking arse. And if you're around there every week asking to borrow a can opener, the chances are you should just buy a fucking can opener (or stop buying tinned goods).

∼

Mind your own fucking business

Try, try and try again. That's the advice given to school children who don't succeed on their first attempt at something trivial, like skipping or spinning a hula hoop or using a potty. It's similar to advice we give teenagers when they're attempting more complex stuff like doing keepy-uppies or driving tests or taking exams, except we don't say it in such a babyish tone of voice. But the best advice for grown-ups involved in neighbourly disputes is not to try, try and try again. It's go home, close your curtains and mind your own fucking business. While it might seem easy on the surface, it's actually quite difficult and a large amount of practice and self-restraint is required.

The danger is that this type of conformity and enforced privacy can potentially lead to some horrific places, which we only ever discover when a house is surrounded by a SWAT team, and news reports inform us that its inhabitants have actually been manufacturing methamphetamine in the basement, or stockpiling weapons in preparation for a zombie apocalypse. We've all seen the bewildered neighbour being interviewed by news crews, saying: 'They seemed like such a normal family – we had no idea he was running Albuquerque's biggest drugs cartel.'

∼

With a bit of luck – and probably a lot of effort – we can get through our days and return home to what vaguely resembles some sort of domestic bliss if you squint your eyes slightly and put your fingers in your ears. The perfect utopian neighbourhood doesn't exist, simply because we all have different ideas of what it should look like. But a harmonious community can be achieved if we're all willing to give and take a bit – next door is only a footstep away, but with a little understanding you can find the perfect blend. (Copyright: Tony Hatch, Jackie Trent, 1984.)

Even if you don't feel compelled to join in with the neighbourhood conformity because you're a punk and fuck-the-system, you can still act on purely selfish reasons. Do something because you might want a favour returned one day in the future; do what you can to help others and you might earn enough 'community points' to be forgiven when you fuck up royally. The problems occur when it's all take and no give, so you shouldn't be surprised if people start treating you like a fucking parasite. (Please note that doing a couple of trivial things such as taking a parcel for a neighbour, or warning them that it's about to rain if their clothes are on the line doesn't entitle you to anything other than a sense of goodwill. It doesn't mean that you're permitted to nip into their hot tub when they're out, or race bangers in the back garden.)

There's an old saying that 'good hedges make good neighbours', and I'd agree. Just make sure they're nicely fucking trimmed once a year.

∾

9. THE ENVIRONMENT

❧

'A society grows great when the old plant trees whose shade they know they shall never sit in.'

Greek proverb

❧

THE ENVIRONMENT

If we take the general gist of good manners to be a way of treating others with respect and consideration, then you hardly need Olympic qualifications to make the leap to doing the same to the world around us. It's there for all of us to enjoy, and just because a generation hasn't yet been born, it doesn't mean we should leave the place looking like the aftermath of a Kate Moss birthday party for them.

In the same way that when you move house it's generally considered good manners to leave the place in as pleasant a state as possible for the next owners, we should apply the same thinking to our current shared residence, earth. Some may take the view that we're perfectly entitled to remove the light fittings, carpets, fireplace, water features and whatever else isn't nailed down, but it doesn't do any good in the long term. Of course the new residents will move in and have their own plans to improve the place – maybe knock through a few walls, rip off the flock wallpaper and upgrade the avocado bathroom set – that's up to them to decide. But trashing the fucking place and leaving everything for the next poor sod to sort out is fairly high on the knobbish behaviour meter.

It's hardly realistic that we should all instantly adopt self-sufficient lifestyles, setting up our own communes, growing crops, singing songs and making our own shoes out of recycled washing-up liquid bottles – we're definitely far too set in our ways for that to happen. But we can all start making small changes towards a more sustainable life – let's face it, we've got a long fucking journey to make, so even talking about it is a step in the right direction.

We all live differently, and whether you're on the lentil-loving-hemp-wearing-chaining-myself-to-a-tree side of things or at the gas-guzzling-burger-chomping-lear-jetting end of the spectrum, we can all make room for a few improvements. It's probably just a little easier for the latter to reduce their impact. The good news is that unlike manners, we can offset our environmental etiquette, giving some leeway for the more lavish lifestyle choices we want to make. Flying to Thailand? Give up meat for a month. Can't live without your four-by-four? Help clean up a beach. Still eating lobster for breakfast? I don't know, plant a fucking forest or something?

The key is creating a balance of give and take, instead of an all-consuming fuck-'em attitude. It's our responsibility to show the next generation that eco-friendly wasn't just a token badge we stuck on laundry detergent, and leave the world as we'd like to find it. It's a lot easier than you might think.

❧

Here's a quick list of a few things to think about if you're interested in showing some fucking good manners to people who you'll quite possibly never meet. But that's not the fucking point:

Don't throw your fucking litter. Don't buy disposable goods. Buy things that are made to last. Don't flick your fucking cigarette butt in the street. Stop buying so much crap. Eat more fucking vegetables. Eat less fucking meat. Stop chucking away perfectly decent food. Buy what you fucking need. Buy more local foods. Buy more seasonal food. Stop buying endless fucking cookery books which need ingredients imported from all over the world such as daikon, jicama and monk's beard. Stop using so much plastic. Or if you're buying plastic, make sure you reuse it and recycle it. Eat less processed food. Get a fucking allotment. Enjoy your time there. Buy a reusable bottle for water and a cup for your caffeine habit. Look after that reusable bottle and coffee cup. Don't fly first class. Enjoy a staycation. Use more public transport (while watching your fucking manners). Take fewer long-haul flights.

Stop taking business trips to the other side of the world when you could probably just send a fucking email. Do some fucking volunteering. Organise a fucking litter pick up in your neighbourhood. Do more walking. Turn your fucking engine off at the school gates. Don't rev your fucking accelerator. Drive responsibly. Get an electric car. Stop buying so much fucking stuff. Stop chucking stuff away after music festivals. (Don't be fooled into thinking it's being sent to a refugee camp and you're actually doing the world a favour.) Make do with what you've got. Look after your shit. Stop buying fast fashion. Buy fewer clothes of better quality. Don't buy this season's must-haves. Don't listen to what 'experts' say on adverts – YOU DO NOT NEED TO RENEW YOUR FUCKING MATTRESS EVERY FIVE YEARS. Stop buying shit just because it's in the sale. Turn the fucking lights off. Turn the fucking heating down. Put on a jumper if you're too cold. Take off a jumper if you're too hot. Buy some energy-efficient light bulbs. Stop buying outdoor-fucking-heaters so you can sit outside until 1am in April. Switch your energy provider. Use green energy. Turn your fucking water heater down. Turn your fucking taps off when you're brushing your teeth. Give stuff to charity. Sell it on eBay or

Gumtree or put it on Freecycle. Stop living like an entitled douchebag who thinks the world is there for your enjoyment only. Pretty please.

In the words of Maximus Decimus Meridius, 'What we do in life, echoes in eternity.' Now, sometimes that thing is really, really epic, like discovering gravity, or inventing the internet, or travelling back through time to save the life of a woman who will give birth to the leader of the resistance and save mankind from the machines. Sometimes it's a bit more normal, but should still be applauded, like teaching a kid to do algebra or helping to build a library. And sometimes that thing is hardly noticeable, like turning off a tap or reusing a plastic bag. I'm not suggesting by any means that at some point in the future a statue will be erected in your honour for doing either of those things, but making a big difference is simply a series of lots of little differences squidged together.

Unless we start doing these seemingly insignificant things then our planet's going to be fucked. It's not about trying to do it all at once, or even having zero impact on the planet – as living human beings we will always have an impact on our planet, and I'm in no way encouraging the alternative. We simply need to redress the balance between giving and taking.

And, if you genuinely couldn't give a fuck about the planet, then at least consider the money you could save.

∾

10. THE WORKPLACE

❧

*'Good manners will open doors that
the best education cannot.'*

CLARENCE THOMAS

❧

THE WORKPLACE

The office is a most irksome world when it comes to finding some fucking good manners. There are general rules to stick to, but there are all sorts of other factors that muddy the proverbial waters, such as what industry you're in, what company you work for and how much of a dipshit your boss is. Ultimately they're the ones who make the rules (or build the culture or write the hymn sheets or whatever terminology they want to use) so if you're doing your best to remain polite, helpful and considerate, but are still left feeling as appreciated as a toilet attendant at Glastonbury, then perhaps you're in the wrong fucking job.

As TV series *The Office* illustrated so beautifully, first in the UK and then the US, it's not always cream that rises to the top – turds can float equally well sometimes. It's too often the case that nice, considerate people get overlooked for promotion in favour of those who are 'more hungry for success'. Which is basically just a polite way of saying they're ruthless, heartless and will pretty much shit on anyone if it helps them get a raise.

Power goes to people's heads, and a group of respectful, hardworking employees can be quickly transformed into a group of rampant, sexist bullies in an attempt to brown-nose the boss. However, the toxic masculinity that has been exposed in so many workplaces in recent years is slowly being replaced by the radical idea that hiring decent, respectful, hardworking people who can demonstrate some fucking good manners, actually produces an environment that people enjoy working in. Who'd have fucking thought it?

As the great philosopher Uncle Ben/Voltaire said: 'With great power comes great responsibility', and a quick search of the web will reveal multiple grades of twatish behaviour from the top dog/big cheese/head honcho:

- The boss who sacked an employee for baking the wrong kind of cupcakes.
- The boss who made the intern buy flowers for his wife, and his mistress.
- The boss who forced two women to kiss each other and broke one's nose in the process.
- The boss who sacked an employee as he lay in a hospital bed after a double heart bypass.
- The boss who sacked her entire restaurant workforce via Facebook.

- The boss who punched her secretary because she was unhappy with the way he'd cut her peach.
- The boss who sacked staff members for disarming an armed robber.
- The boss who sacked his employee for serving him flat cola.

And, of course, we have the example set by the boss of the free world, who thinks it's acceptable to grab women 'by the pussy', mock handicapped people, allegedly pay off sex workers and refer to Mexicans as rapists. I don't want to get too political in this book, but I'm just saying that as an example to set, it's not great. (In the interests of balancing things out, the UK's former Prime Minister David Cameron allegedly put his tallywhacker in the mouth of a severed pig's head. So I think the UK takes that round on points.)

It's difficult to tell how many of these 'bosses' are real or just hypothetical figures made up by online recruitment companies to create content for their websites. But most people have heard first-hand some sort of horror story of bosses abusing their power, and when the person at the top is behaving like a prize dick, it creates a few more than 50 shades of grey as to what is and isn't acceptable. Each workplace environment usually finds its own happy (ish) level of tolerance, but when you're starting out it can be tricky to adapt to that culture – if you even want to at all.

Everyone has to work there, from Jaimie – the narcissistic young hipster who's just changed his LinkedIn profile to incorporate the word 'entrepreneur' in every sentence, to Claire – the gossip who has issues with germs and leaves passive-aggressive Post-its in the kitchen. It's highly unlikely that it's ever going to be the perfect place for everyone – or anyone – but we can try to treat each other with respect and act in a professional manner that ensures some degree of harmony. At least until the office party when everyone gets pissed and decides to say what they really think.

❧

Do your fucking homework

It's a global economy. We work in different time zones, with people from different countries and cultures. It shouldn't come as too much of a fucking surprise that not everyone will appreciate being high-fived at the start of a meeting. If you're lucky enough to be flown across the world to have a meeting with a client, then do a bit of fucking research on what business customs are favoured or frowned upon in their country.

~

Learn people's fucking names

Not being able to pronounce someone's name doesn't make you racist, it just means you have difficulty saying a word you've never fucking seen before. Understanding the subtle inflections and silent letters of another language is complicated, because it's Another. Fucking. Language. Journalists have weeks to prepare for their commentary and still spend hours debating how to pronounce Ole Gunnar Solskjær, Mesut Özil, Wojciech Szczęsny or Sokratis Papastathopoulos. If you're in doubt, take time to check how it's pronounced and spelled correctly, and apologise for any future mistakes. If you do have a name that people have difficulty with then please don't take offence if they get it wrong – help them get it right.

~

Treat everyone equally

Just because you earn more money in the time it takes to have your morning constitutional than someone else does in a month, it doesn't give you the right to treat them like a subservient leper. Everyone has their job to do, whether it's making tea, mopping floors or just going from meeting room to meeting room intimidating people. You're all on the same fucking team, hopefully heading in the same direction, so treat them with the same respect – say please and thank you and excuse me. As comedian/musician/writer Tim Minchin says: 'I don't care if you're the most powerful cat in the room, I will judge you on how you treat the least powerful. So there.'

❧

Make some fucking effort with your clothes
Most offices have some form of dress code. If you're in the painting and decorating industry it's likely to be a little more relaxed than if you work in corporate hospitality. But even if you've no idea what you're doing, you can at least make an attempt to look like you do and give the impression that you want to work there. If you're up for an interview then dress smart, and for fuck's sake clean your shoes.

❧

Take your fucking sunglasses off

Always when you're indoors. Especially if you're talking to someone. Even if you're currently earning more than $20 million per film. Unless you have some sort of visual impairment, obviously.

∼

Learn some fucking elevator etiquette

There are many rules that can be found on the subject, but the main things to avoid are: holding the doors open to finish a conversation; talking on your fucking mobile phone; talking over the top of someone; having your music on too loud; eating food; not facing the doors and staring straight ahead; not letting people off when it's their floor. And farting, obviously.

∼

Say what you fucking mean

The business world is full of ugly acronyms, obscure abbreviations and bullshitty jargon, generally designed to make people feel more intelligent than they are. It started with thinking outside the box, putting ducks in rows and hitting the ground running, but each workplace has its own unique set of bullshit buzzwords. Levels are so high now that it's perfectly common to sit through whole meetings without having a fucking clue what people are talking about. Forget about running things up the flagpole and touching base and getting the ball rolling and peeling back the fucking onion. Stop wasting people's time with this gibberish and start using some plain fucking English.

∼

Mind your fucking language

Yes, you might think this is a bit rich coming as advice in a book riddled with potty words, but this isn't a workplace. Once you're inside the four walls of the office then you need to accept that not everyone's so comfortable with your colourful use of language, so set your censorship mode to PG or perhaps 12A. Workplaces are pretty high-stress environments, so when things do go tits-up then an outburst of expletives is often tolerated, but it's best not to do this in full view of the company. Find a private and hopefully well sound-proofed room, unleash the barrage of Malcolm Tucker-esque vocabulary, take a deep breath, count to ten and get back to work.

∼

Don't be fucking late

While the fabulous technological advances in the last twenty years have made it abundantly quicker and easier to do business, the end result is that we try to cram more and more stuff into our days in an effort to appear more productive. We fill our nine-to-five with emails and meetings and meetings about meetings and oh-fuck-it-I'll-skip-lunch-and-have-a-sandwich-at-my-desk, so it's only natural to try and cut a few minutes here and there to have a quick whiz because you haven't been in six hours. But time, as we are constantly reminded by those folk who collate our hours, is money, and being late generally suggests to those waiting that your time is more valuable than everyone else's. If you're the boss, then obviously everyone has to wait for you and no one can really complain about you being late. But you can still show some fucking manners and apologise – even if you don't really mean it.

~

Learn some fucking humility

In the corporate world we're all keen to gain some recognition for what we've achieved – to blow our own trumpets and show the boss just how deserving we are of that window office/generous pay rise/

car upgrade. If your boss is any good they should recognise this, but don't go blabbing on about how you fucking restocked the paper in the photocopier or unloaded the dishwasher because you didn't have a cup.

If you feel that something worthy of a medal has been overlooked then make a note of it and bring it up at the appropriate time, rather than sending an all-staff email telling everyone what a fucking good job you did.

∾

Don't take all the fucking credit

Worse than the bilious self-promoting numpties are the group of swinging-dicks who feel no shame in taking the credit for other people's efforts. The ones who reluctantly help out a little and then exaggerate their role in proceedings once it's been deemed a success. Get a grip of yourself and give praise to those who genuinely deserve it.

∾

Introduce yourself properly

A first impression says a lot about you, so make it count. You don't need to come across as all macho with overly vigorous handshakes and back pats and big grins – this can be just as awkward, as Donald Trump's nineteen-second handshake with Japanese Prime Minister Shinzō Abe proved so well. Or his 29-second shake with Emmanuel Macron.

Of course, if he was meeting Jioji Konrote, the President of Fiji, this behaviour would be positively encouraged. As mentioned before, different cultures have different greetings, so make sure you brush up on what's to be expected, whether it's handshakes or bowing or high-fives or double-cheek air kisses with left leg raised backwards from the knee. Equally important is saying your name. Even if you've met once or twice before you can make it fucking easier for everyone and remove any awkward moments of silence. And stand up when you fucking shake someone's hand.

∼

Put your fucking phone away

There was a time when people would use their phones as a sign of how important and busy they were. Today, in a world where we're all on multiple platforms of Facebook, Twitter, Instagram, LinkedIn and WhatsApp it seems the opposite is true, and having a phone out in a meeting is seen as a clear indication that the fucking phone is more important than anyone else in the room. Put it the fuck away and you'll find the meeting is much more productive. Not just on the table or face down in front of you. Away, where no one can see it. And don't be fooled into thinking that no one notices you checking it under the table.

Around the office correct mobile etiquette is equally important to maintain a degree of tranquillity with your fellow workmates. Put it on silent, and, if it happens to start vibrating in your pocket while you're talking to someone, then say excuse me before checking who's calling. Whether you answer it is probably just a judgement call on who you're talking to at the time. *Hint: if you're talking to your boss, don't answer it.*

∾

Don't fucking interrupt

There are many degrees of interruption, depending on who's talking, the style of conversation, the perceived power between the two, and what they're talking about. There are some perfectly acceptable ways in which two people can talk at the same time without it being rude. The interruption I'm referring to is the 'Fuck off, you're wrong, I'm right' interruption, also known as the 'I'm more fucking important than you' interruption. In some board-rooms this is passed off as healthy 'debate', but the problem in business is there's rarely a person to keep the overblown, shouty opinions in check, and many decisions are made purely on the basis of who's got the biggest fucking gob.

Once someone's started to say something then let them fucking finish before you come blazing in with your interjection. You never know, you might learn something. Like, you're wrong. Or maybe you're right, but at least let them finish their fucking sentence. If you're really desperate to say something you think needs to be addressed, then raise a hand and let the person speaking bring you into the discussion.

～

Take it fucking easy at the office party

Whether it's celebrating a new contract, the retirement of a long-serving employee you never met, or the annual festive gathering, the office party rarely fails to disappoint when it comes to raised eyebrows and sore heads. Alcohol is the main cause of this, as hair is let down, tongues are loosened and inhibitions tossed to the side as freely as a pair of pants at a swingers night, but you need to know your fucking limits. Shots come out and the quiet girl from accounts can soon be found gyrating with a hoover; the old dude from finance reveals his twerking skills; an unknown person is sick in the filing cabinet; the boss does his best not to do anything that may be later used in court against him.

What degree of humiliation awaits you once you make it into the office the next day depends on a variety of factors, including the number of people who saw intimate parts of your body and how many people were filming at the time. But all of it can be avoided by just going easy on the booze.

∿

Leave the kitchen clean and fucking tidy
The kitchen is an area for everyone to use. Some like tea and coffee. Others prefer a bit of toast in the morning. As our days are increasingly jammed with extra shit to do and our dietary requirements become more and more fastidious, it's not uncommon to be greeted by a scene from *Hell's Kitchen* at lunchtime. But whether you're making a brew or a banquet, the one rule you need to follow is to tidy up your shit afterwards. It doesn't matter what your paygrade is, leave the kitchen clean and fucking tidy for the next person to use. Even if you've got

someone who's paid to clear up, you can at least show them the courtesy of putting a plate in the dishwasher or washing up a fucking teaspoon.

❧

Get your own fucking food

As we attempt to turn lunch hour into an episode of *Come Dine with Me*, the kitchen cupboards tend to get clogged up with remnants of these meals. Some are more protective of these items than others – bottles of ketchup or mayonnaise, a tub of lacto-free butter or half an avocado can be left for ages without being used. But ultimately you have to respect the fact that if you didn't fucking pay for it, you shouldn't fucking take it. Ask around, by all means, but don't nick someone else's. Equally, if you do appear to have more food in the office than in your own kitchen, then perhaps think about taking some of it home and giving everyone else a bit more space for theirs.

❧

Don't cook fucking stinky foods

If you do insist on bringing fish, eggs, broccoli, burgers or any other stinky food into the office, you have to accept the side-order of abuse that will most likely come your way. This isn't corporate bullying, or any other kind of harassment other than a legitimate response to you stinking the fucking place out.

❧

Keep the fucking noise down

The exact level depends on your individual workplace and who's in close proximity to you, but you need to accept that if your own personal (and possibly unnecessary) habits are interfering with other people doing their work, it's going to cause some issues. It shouldn't get to the point of everyone treading on eggshells for every minute of the day, but check to see if others can hear Hootie and the Blowfish blasting out through your headphones, and don't use the fucking speakerphone unless you've got your own sound-proofed office. If you want to chat in an open plan office then walk around and talk face-to-face rather than shout through the partitions or 'prairie-dog' over the top.

❧

Mind your personal fucking space

It's not only intrusive noises that can wind up co-workers; giving them a respectable amount of personal space is equally important. For some this might mean taking a step back when you talk to them, allowing for the successful diffusion of any undigested breakfast; for others it may mean tidying all the shit on your desk up at the end of the day. People are incredibly sensitive about being cramped for personal space – it's tolerated on the tube or in crowds, but in the office you can't help but question someone's motives for getting so close. Even if it doesn't come across as creepy, it can be a little awkward from an olfactory point of view.

∽

Give their fucking seat back

The office isn't a place to play musical fucking chairs. If you borrow someone's seat while they're away from their desk so you can chat to their neighbour, it is your obligation to get the fuck out of it when they return. Not when you've finished the conversation, or when they say 'Do you mind if I have my seat back?' It doesn't matter how senior you are or how junior they might be – it's their fucking seat so get out of it.

∽

Don't hog the air con

Life in the office can get heated sometimes, ironically due to the endless power struggle over the fucking air con. One person's perfect ambient temperature for working is rarely the same as someone else's, but before you storm aggressively to the control panel, take a second to see if you could put on a jumper or remove a layer, and if not, then ask politely if anyone minds you changing it. Hopefully you can find a happy medium.

∾

Learn to use the fucking internet

We should all be in agreement that everyone's pretty fucking busy from nine to five, and no one's really looking for extra jobs to do. So before you interrupt someone with a fairly inane question about pig milk or vegan-friendly fossil fuels, ask yourself if you could answer it yourself by using the fucking internet. Use your initiative to work out if it's actually better to let everyone else get on with their work, instead of doing your job.

∾

Put the fucking kettle on

Hot drinks are an essential part of most offices around the world. Caffeine is generally the preferred drug of choice to fuel our days, but increasingly we're seeing a wider range of herbal alternatives, many of them with the power to increase/decrease metabolism, reduce flatulence, restore energy, aid focus and see into the future. Whatever your hot drink of choice is, the rule is if someone makes you a drink, you return the fucking favour later. Don't convince yourself that no one noticed you making a cup of selfish, because they did, and they silently hate you, and one day that silent hate may become a non-silent hate, and then it turns ugly. All because you didn't have the common decency to make someone a fucking cup of tea. Sometimes you get a shit round when everyone wants a brew; sometimes you can time it cleverly so you get the credit for asking, but no one else wants one. But you have to fucking ask.

Also, please note that an offer of drinks (in an office) does not cover off the full Starbucks menu, so try and limit your requests to basic ones that involve hot water, milk, sugar and maybe sweeteners. Requests for strength and colour chart references are pretentiously twatish and therefore reserved for senior management.

∼

Stay at fucking home
Once you enter the world of full-time employment you're deemed mature and responsible enough to

diagnose whether you're fit enough to go into work if you're ill. Sadly this decision is often clouded by many other factors, such as how urgent a meeting is, and how many days off you've already taken pretending you were ill, when you were just hungover. If you are under the weather with something contagious, do the right thing and stay at home rather than spreading your fucking germs around the office so everyone else gets sick.

∾

A lot of these 'rules' for employment etiquette are based on a fairly typical office job, but it's never as simple as that. There are so many different types of work – from cleaning shark tanks and pushing people on to trains, to tasting dog food and fluffing pandas – that require their own individual set of rules. Many workplaces now have their own code of conduct that's built into their contracts, and that can vary depending on the kind of culture the boss is trying to nurture.

Whatever the general vibe of your workplace is, you need to use some common-fucking-sense and display some tolerance to your fellow employees. You don't have to see eye-to-eye on everything; you don't have to be BFFs or part of the office book club.

No one wants a room full of clones dutifully nodding their heads and patting each other on the back – this type of behaviour is what leads to such toxic workplaces in the first place, as little cliques and clubs are formed. But what you should always do is accept that the perfect job is a rare thing indeed, and you need to pick your battles carefully. But if you hate going to work; no one respects you; you wish you were someone else; you cry constantly; you daydream of punching small animals and you sit next to a guy who works in his pants and picks his toenails, it may be time to quit. As a rule. (Hats tipped to the Wieden & Kennedy creative department.)

Which brings us nicely on to one final rule:

༄

Say goodbye nicely

The internet is full of spectacular ways to quit your job – hilarious and creative ideas to stick it to the bastards who have made your life a fucking misery for the last five years. The temptation to let them know exactly how you feel by handing in your notice dressed as a banana, or accompanied by a marching band, or with a hilarious video that makes you a YouTube sensation for 24 hours, can be too much for some to resist. But you also have the opportunity to show some integrity and dignity. To take the moral high ground and demonstrate that no matter how shit they may have made your life, you won't be lowered to their level. Much like a single-digit gesture to the a-hole driver who has just cut you up, it may result in some short-term satisfaction, and possibly a few likes and LOLs on social media, but leave holding your head high, not your middle finger. You never know when it might come back to haunt you.

∾

11. EMAILS

~

'Evil communication corrupts good manners. I hope to live to hear that good communication corrects bad manners.'

BENJAMIN BANNEKER

~

EMAILS

Email is a most useful invention. Equally, it's a pain in the fucking arse. Invented by Ray Tomlinson back in the sixties, our reliance on email has ballooned over recent years and it's now estimated that we spend about a quarter of our working week reading, writing, deciphering and deleting the fucking things. Whether it's from a colleague, an old friend, an exclusive 50 per cent off the thing you just bought, or a once-in-a-lifetime opportunity to inherit a fortune from an unknown prince in a remote part of the world, email has taken over our lives. There's not much you can do without it these days, but as our dependence on it has gone upwards, so has our understanding of how it can be abused.

As useful as it is to prove to your boss that they did promise you a pay rise three years ago, it also serves as proof of your slightly misjudged sense of humour ten years ago. Our digital footprints are there for anyone with an advanced knowledge of computer hacking to share with the world, and once they're out in the open, you need a fairly shit-hot PR company to limit the damage. Years of charity work and image-building can be undone with a leaked email that calls the UK honours system a 'fucking joke' just because you were overlooked for a knight-hood. And there's one of the big problems: writing the words 'it's a fucking joke' can be interpreted in so many different ways, depending on how you want to read it. Picture a well-respected ex-England football captain sat at his home computer, tears in his eyes, head in his hands as his wife looks scornfully over his shoulder. He types the words 'It's a fucking joke.' Now picture the same player sat on the floor in his pants, surrounded by empty beer bottles (possibly Becks, but other brands are available) with rage in his eyes as he beats his fingers against the keyboard and types 'It's a fucking joke.' Or, it could be that he was just happily sunbathing on the beach, laughing with his family and quickly replied while a waiter was taking his cocktail order. The words are still the same, but the interpretation can be wildly different.

Hillary Clinton, Ivanka Trump, Sarah Palin, Johnny Depp, George Clooney and a host of other A- to Z-listers have all been exposed by having private emails made public, and from that point on it doesn't matter what you meant, only the words that you wrote.

But let's get away from the glitz and glamour and back to the common-or-garden-variety office. Just because *OK!* magazine has never heard of us, doesn't mean that we're immune from having our personal thoughts splashed across the glossies. Here are five stories that so beautifully illustrate why you should never email anyone anything that you wouldn't want printed on the front page. I've removed their names because, let's face it, they've probably suffered enough, and gossiping's hardly fucking good manners.

1) The graduate at Deloitte who wrote a Christmas list of awards, including 'boy most likely to sleep his way to the top' and 'most attractive older member of staff'.[18] It's hardly scandalous, but by the time it had spread to Australia and been read by a few million people, it was time for her to move on.

2) The senior associate at one of the world's biggest law firms who demanded his secretary cover the cost of a £4 dry cleaning bill after she just got back from her mother's funeral. How she was the cause of the ketchup stain was never made clear, but it ended with a giant shitstorm and the associate resigning from his six-figure salary job.

3) The investment banker who decided to email his mates back home to let them know how good life was in Korea. By 'good life' the words he actually used were 'fuck every hot chick in Korea over the next two years'. Sadly this good life came to a premature

155

end when one of his mates forwarded the email, and within 24 hours his not-so-humblebragging was being ridiculed by millions worldwide. Probably including a fair percentage of the 'hot chicks' in Korea.

4) The pair of legal secretaries in Sydney, Australia, who ended up in a full on, reply-all war of words, while the rest of the company grabbed some popcorn and settled in for the show. The first email was a mildly passive-aggressive note asking for the return of a ham sandwich and some cheese. The reply was a reasonably polite note to enquire if she'd checked the correct fridge. The mistake was she replied all, and from there on things descended pretty rapidly. The ensuing tête-à-tête included some true old-school bitchiness, including such classics as 'Being a brunette doesn't mean you're smart though!', 'Miss Can't Keep A Boyfriend' and the somewhat unusual sucker punch of 'I have five guys at the moment! haha.'[19] Needless to say both lost their jobs and the whereabouts of the ham sandwich remains a mystery to this day.

5) And finally, as if you need any more proof that emailing personal messages is a bad idea, spare a thought for the lady who was generous enough to email her boyfriend congratulating him on the superior taste of his semen. Sadly he decided to

forward his five-star review on to friends and soon her correspondence was being shared by pretty much anyone who had internet access back in 2001. 'Yummy' was the exact adjective she chose, but the global publicity that ensued had a slightly more bitter taste.

For every one of these major mishaps, there must be a few thousand minor ones that have been consigned to the depths of the internet somewhere. It's all too easy for someone to save it in a folder, hit 'forward' or take a screen grab, so treat your email with respect and caution. Take time to compose them properly and always sleep on any contentious issues before sending a reply. If in doubt, go and speak to them in person. (Just make sure they're not recording the conversation.)

∼

Learn how to fucking spell

Reading an email with spelling mistakes is like talking to someone with bad breath. It's perfectly understandable, and human, and one or two whiffs can be ignored, but it's pretty grim if every fucking sentence stinks. Autocorrect is often the culprit for these errors – a few years back my computer decided I was more likely to use the word 'willies' than I was 'wellies', much to the amusement of the recipient when I mentioned how 'the kids all had muddy willies'. Too many spelling mistakes give the impression that you've rushed your words and didn't think it through properly – the main reason why internet trolls are picked up on their poor grasp of the English language: if you can't spell or use a fucking apostrophe correctly then your opinion doesn't fucking count. Typos will inevitably creep in, but if you want people to take you seriously, you need to do some serious checking.

∽

Get to the fucking point

We're all pushed for time. So keep your email simple. Don't put in too much waffle. Make it clear what you're asking. That doesn't mean you can't do a quick informal intro. Hope all's well. Thanks for sending that over. That sort of stuff. But if it looks too long to read, there's a good chance it won't be read. So keep it simple.

∽

Cut the comedy

If you're writing a personal email to a personal friend, from a personal email address, then by all means make it personal. Put in as many LOLs and ROFLs and fucking LMAOs as you feel comfortable with. Presumably if they're a friend then they know you well enough to make a decent judgement on the tone you're taking, and are unlikely to forward it on to the world's press. (Just be careful not to brag too much about your lavish new lifestyle in Korea.) But in the workplace humour does not translate so well, particularly if you're a fan of irony or sarcasm. Emojis can help clarify your precise tone (as can exclamation marks!!!!!!!) but neither have a place in a respectable business email. 'But they're so sweet and clever!' you say? I don't care if it's just one teeny-tiny fucking winky smiley face, once you open the doors to emojis you're setting a dangerous precedent. Before you know it you'll be sending those little face-palm ones or a pile of poo with eyes, so you've got to draw the line somewhere. Save your reputation as office comedian for face-to-face encounters, where you can use actual emotions to get across how you feel.

∼

Check your fucking recipients

Pause. Count to five. Take those five seconds to check exactly who you're about to send that email to. Even if you send over 100 emails a day, those combined 500 seconds (8.33 minutes) each day could help you keep the job you've worked so hard to get. The Reply All button is the cause of most irritation and embarrassment, especially if it's a snarky comment about the previous email. But even if it's not, you should have a think about whether all 500 employees need to hear your opinions. It's not an exact science, but if there are fewer than ten people on the list, you can reply all; more than ten and you should probably just reply to the sender, unless specified.

∾

Check your content

As outlined earlier, you need to be careful what you write these days. Most advice is in the region of 'Don't write it if you wouldn't want your mother to read it' but seeing as some mums can be fairly liberal these days it's perhaps safer to stick to 'Don't write it if you wouldn't want it printed on the front page of a newspaper'. But you have to be equally careful to make sure there's nothing already existing in an email chain that might cause offence. When there are multiple people cc'd and many messages are flying backwards and forwards, just double-check that there's nothing mentioned in an earlier email that could land you – or someone else – in shit creek.

❧

Just be fucking patient

Back in the pre-email days your communication options were phone or letter. The former normally got an immediate response – if they were in; the latter would take a couple of days. Emails are instant; however don't misguidedly assume that this warrants an instant fucking reply. You've no idea of what the recipient is doing when your email pinged into their inbox, so unless you've mentioned otherwise, give them at least 48 hours before following up with a passive-aggressive 'Just checking you got my last email?' note. Text messages have a similar window of about 48 hours for responses, but for Facebook messages the window can be anything between six months and the rest of your life.

Similarly, sending an email late at night or on weekends is absolutely fine – the introduction of flexible working hours means not everyone works a traditional nine-to-five. But to expect someone to read and reply to it in the same timescale shows an epic fucking lack of respect.

❧

Just fucking say sorry

If you don't manage to reply in time, or you feel you've breeched your own personal time limit, then a simple 'Sorry for the delay' or 'Apologies for the late response' never hurts. Accept these apologies gracefully and move on.

While we're on the subject of replying, in the business world it's generally considered a smidge inconsiderate to reply via a different medium. If they send an email, reply via email, text to text, WhatsApp to WhatsApp, carrier pigeon to carrier pigeon. It's just being professional.

❧

There are many other suggestions for email etiquette, ranging from 'Don't use "Yo" as an introduction', to what font you should use, but to my mind a lot of these can vary depending on who you're email-ing and how well you know them. As funky young start-ups attempt to make the workplace a more in-formal environment with a selection of playground slides, ball pools, bean bags and garden sheds, so the tone of emails can drift into equally informal waters. Not every correspondence needs to be drafted as if you're writing to royalty, but the general rule should be that if it's a professional email, then keep it professional. Remember: an email is for life, and there's every chance of it being taken out of context and over-analysed in years to come.

᷈

12. SOCIAL MEDIA

❧

'Don't believe everything you read on the internet just
because there's a picture with a quote next to it.'

ABRAHAM LINCOLN

❧

SOCIAL MEDIA

If the transport system is the Wild West of the etiquette world, then the internet is what leading scientists and sociologists are increasingly referring to as 'a right fucking mess'. Adoption of words like 'troll' suggest that there are more than a few dark and murky corners of the online world that display some rather dubious consideration towards other people's feelings. Online shaming, cyber bullying, revenge porn, doxing, fake news and scamming are all part of a savage universe where private lives are made public for all to cast judgement on, and whole reputations can be destroyed with a few rushed and badly thought through tags and tweets.

The whole concept of freedom of speech has been brought into question as hate speech rears its ugly head across multiple platforms, and social media sites are increasingly facing pressure to clean up their content, whether they believe they're responsible for it or not. Where exactly the line lies between expressing your personal opinions and spreading extremist views is a complicated question. Hate speech is equally difficult to define, whether it's in a leaked private email, a Facebook group set up by a political adviser or a parody Twitter account that makes fun of social justice warriors. What is clear though, is that things have got pretty out of fucking control in recent times. As touched on earlier, there is always someone, somewhere who will take offence to pretty much anything, unless we start living in a world where we suppress genuine beliefs and opinions – however misguided they may be – and just post pictures of cats and hotdog legs and babies. (Although too many of these can cause similar levels of aggro.) As Jon Ronson says in his book *So You've Been Publicly Shamed*: 'We were creating a world where the smartest way to survive is to be bland.'

The exact number of hours uploaded to YouTube each day varies depending on which source you prefer, but it's safe to say it's somewhere between fuckloads and fuck-me-that's-insane. (YouTube CEO Susan Wojcicki stated in 2015 it was about 400 hours per minute, or 576,000 hours per day, but didn't clarify how much of that content is cat-related.) Now that so many of us are walking CCTV systems, anything vaguely out of the ordinary that catches our eye is instantly snapped or filmed, perhaps out of curiosity, perhaps out of a sense of justice, perhaps so you can flog it to one of the tabloids. (WE PAY CASH FOR YOUR VIDEOS!!!)

The ability to make a living through views and clicks and ad revenue seems to have destroyed all sense of what's fucking appropriate and acceptable. Just have a flick through the 'Most watched' section of any online newspaper and you'll see examples of how we're increasingly obsessed with other people's stupidity/bad manners/anti-social behaviour/mind-blowing fuckwittery. It gives us a perverse sense of schadenfreude to remind ourselves that no matter how grim we think our lives may be – no matter how bad our own manners are – we'd never dare put a cat in a fucking recycling bin or pose naked on top of a sacred mountain in Malaysia. Our desire to share has turned into a demand to shame.

Monica Lewinsky knows a thing or two about having your private life made public. In her TED lecture of March 2015, 'The Price of Shame', she describes herself as 'Patient Zero of losing a personal reputation on a global scale almost instantaneously.' She talks at length about online shaming and the problems it's causing in our society, most notably that: 'A marketplace has emerged where public humiliation is a commodity and shame is an industry.'[20]

This mob-mentality to shame anyone who steps out of line is further fuelled by our ability to remain anonymous on the internet. (Or at least until the police track your IP address and turn up at your front door.) The temptation to 'own', 'school' or 'burn' someone we've probably never met and know very little about, with a #savage (!!!!) put-down is rationalised by a feeling that we're delivering a form of social justice on behalf of the world. Except one person's idea of what's #savage (!!!!) banter tends to vary a great deal from someone else's, and can come across as #justplainfuckingrude.

Fuck Dunbar's rule of 150 people. Grab your digital pitch-forks and your digital flaming torches and let's head down to the digital pillory to throw some rotten digital food at some digital pariah. The more anonymous strangers joining in and publicly venting their outrage the bigger the spectacle becomes, and as with comedy, there's always someone willing to take it several steps too far, elevating nasty words into death threats. We've moved from social media to anti-social media in the time it takes to write 140 characters.

So where does that leave us all? Well the rules of online etiquette (netiquette) are perhaps unsurprisingly rather similar to the way you'd behave offline (or IRL, if you prefer) with the focus on restraint, compassion and empathy. But other than 'never say something online that you wouldn't say to someone's face', what else can we look for? A lot will depend on exactly which corner of the internet you're playing in, but whether you're on Twitter, Facebook, LinkedIn or the *MailOnline* comments section, perhaps the hardest lesson to teach ourselves is this:

❧

Keep your fucking mouth shut

I'm well aware of the irony/hypocrisy of a book that comments on people's behaviour advising others not to comment on people's behaviour, but the best thing we can do is stay out of the fucking argument. Fine if you want to add something positive, but, as so many parents have said over the years, if you don't have anything nice to say then don't say anything at all.

It's not that your opinion doesn't matter, more that your comment will almost definitely be taken out of context and inflame the situation even more. As with the school bully who wanders around the playground tripping people up and handing out wedgies, the best course of action is just to ignore them. As 'Miss Manners' herself (aka Judith Martin) says: 'Dishonesty is not the only alternative to honesty. There is also the highly underrated virtue of shutting up.'

❧

Stop posting every fucking minute

OK. You've had a baby. That's fantastic and possibly/probably/hopefully the greatest fucking thing you've ever done in your life. This should be celebrated with a collection of likes, hearts and various forms of smiley/laughing faces. Or perhaps you went on a really fucking expensive holiday to Costa Rica, or have been helping orphans in Botswana, or just #havingaslide in the Alps. This is great. We fucking get it. But we get it the first time. The second time's perhaps a helpful reminder. The third time is likely to be met with a few flippant comments and severely reduced like-ability. After that we're just fucking bored and can't help but think you'd rather be on Facebook than wherever you are in the world.

No matter how interesting you might think your life is, please restrain your humblebragging. (And under no circumstances should it be acceptable to refer to yourself as an 'influencer'.)

❧

Stop fucking sharing everything you read

At the time of writing Facebook's a little over fifteen years old. Set up on 4 February 2004, most of the early years were spent finding old friends, posting holiday pictures, stalking exes and LOL-ing at cat pics. All these things are still popular pastimes, but more recently (especially post-2016) we've become increasingly more likely to share political opinion by linking newspaper articles. You're never more than a couple of scrolls from another (perhaps well-written) piece on fishing regulations or some collective mourning for another celebrity who's been found dead in a hotel room. But just because you've got a 'Newsfeed', it doesn't mean you're a fucking news channel. Whatever your political persuasion or personal agenda, please share these things in moderation rather than just spamming it willy-fucking-nilly.

∼

Check your fucking facts

Fake news was word of the year in 2017, but it's been around for decades. Most of it was easy to spot because it came from *The News of The World* or *The National Enquirer* and normally featured Richard Gere, Prince Philip, Russia, Sporty Spice, some rodents, alien abduction, lizard heads, Nazi groups, cocaine, Pablo Escobar or the Pope. Or a combination of all of the above. Nowadays it's a little harder to spot and comes from pretty much everywhere (although much of it seems to originate from a small town in Macedonia). If you repost something, you have a responsibility to check the fucking facts first rather than just hit retweet and add a #RIPBeyonce.

∾

Don't 'like' yourself

Put an OMG face on your sister's holiday pics; a LOL emoji on your friend's hilarious video of a dog drinking coffee; a little heart on your workmate's news that she's pregnant, or an angry face on their Brexit post. But whatever you do, don't like your own fucking post. Thank you.

∾

Censor your PD-fucking-As

Love is a beautiful thing. Like raindrops on roses, bright copper kettles, warm woollen mittens and crisp apple strudels, it should be celebrated and enjoyed. But much like offline public displays of affection, online PDAs can cause similar levels of spontaneous vomiting. Maybe a simple message on an anniversary, or a birthday post with some cutesy heart emojis, but daily/weekly/monthly updates on how fucking blessed you are, starts to sound a little psychotic. Show some love; share some love. But do it without the tongues and slurping noises and hands groping all over the fucking place.

∼

Watch your fucking hashtags

Hashtags are fine. Two or three? That's all you need. Five starts to get a little bit confused and messy, and anything above that is completely fucking unnecessary. Hashtags that are well past their best-before date and starting to stink the place out include: #blessed #sorrynotsorry #instagood #squadgoals #foodporn #fitspo #luckygirl #luckyguy #jollybobs #welljel #winning #YOLO #justsaying #truestory #toocute #likeforlike and #noms.

Honourable mentions (via *Sabotage Times*[21]) to make sure you take a little extra care with your hashtags in the future include:

Research In Motion's (aka RIM's) employment push – #RIMjobs

The Chester Literary Festival – #CLitFest

PowerGen's Italian branch – #powergenitalia

And the classic from Susan Boyle's PR company launching her new album – #susanalbumparty

~

Ask before you tag someone

Unless you've already made a verbal agreement that it's OK, don't tag everyone in a picture. Not all of them will have their privacy settings to block/confirm tags, so your default position should always be to ask first. If you can't be fucking bothered to ask, then don't fucking bother to tag them.

~

Keep private/personal views private

They might be called 'Friends' on Facebook, but that's most likely because it sounds better than 'People you know' or 'Random humans you met on holiday eight years ago'. Even though you do technically know them, it's not a private place for private views any more – it's a public place where people shouldn't be subjected to the intimate details of your marriage breakdown or how your new boss is a bit of a pervert. It's not that no one cares, just that a fairly high proportion of your 'friends' couldn't give two fucks and you've turned your life into spam. Of course you want to share what's important to you, but social media is a great way to tell a little to a lot; real life is a great way to tell a lot to a little. (I know it's technically 'to a few', but it doesn't sound so catchy like that.) Choose quality of conversation over quantity every fucking time.

~

Stop checking in

Places that you should avoid 'Checking in' to include: hospitals, airports, funeral homes, posh restaurants, sporting venues or anywhere that's a vain attempt for people to ask: 'Oooo where are you off to?' or 'Hope you're OK, hun.' In fact, just don't fucking bother checking in to anywhere. It's annoying as fuck.

~

Unfriend your non-friends

Should the constant baby pics, holiday updates, political spam, displays of affection become too much then just unfriend or unfollow them. You can now 'mute' most people, which avoids future awkward conversations, but should you find yourself unfriended then don't take it as a personal insult and demand an explanation, for two reasons:

1) You probably don't want to hear the explanation.

2) It doesn't fucking matter.

Everyone should have an annual clear-out of their friends, not because you don't like them necessarily, but simply because you don't have to be friends with everyone you meet. If you do have such a clear-out then you don't have to fucking announce it to the world. Just fucking get on with it.

❧

TURN YOUR FUCKING CAPS LOCK OFF

CAPITAL LETTERS ARE FOR SHOUTING. WRITING NORMAL SENTENCES WITH CAPS LOCK MAKES YOU SEEM LIKE A REALLY ANGRY PERSON.

WRITING IN CAPS LOCK AND BOLD IS EVEN MORE FURIOUS.

<u>AND UNDERLINING IT IS RESERVED FOR EXCLUSIVE USE BY A FEW EXTRA SPECIAL *MAILONLINE* READERS.</u>

Use lower case words to sound like you haven't lost all fucking sense of reality.

❧

Put your fucking phone away (at concerts)

Or your tablet or GoPro thingy. Just enjoy what you're doing in real life without having to think about when you're going to upload it, what fucking hashtags and filters you should use, or what pithy comment will get the most likes. Take some pictures, get a selfie with the Mrs and leave it at that, but don't spend two hours at a concert holding your oversized fucking iPad in the air and blocking everyone else's view. Use your own eyes to remember the event, rather than use it as an excuse to tell everyone where you were/how much fun you had.

❧

Stop posting fucking selfies

It was on 2 March 2014 that Ellen DeGeneres gathered Hollywood pals around her at the 86th Academy Awards for the world's most famous selfie. There was Brad and Angelina, Bradley and Jennifer, Lupita and Peter, Meryl, Julia, and Kevin lurking ominously at the back. It's now estimated there are over 1,000 selfies uploaded to Instagram every ten seconds and they've become so popular (or unpopular, depending on your viewpoint) that many places have now banned the use of selfie sticks, including Disneyland, the Sistine Chapel and the Coachella Festival. Nearly two-thirds of Americans admit to taking one (YouGov, August 2018) but we need to stop doing it Every. Fucking. Time. Moderate your narcissism, please, and note that it's never acceptable to take a selfie at a funeral. Something that former Danish Prime Minister Helle Thorning-Schmidt could have noted when she took a selfie with David Cameron and Barack Obama at a memorial for Nelson Mandela in 2013.

∾

Ignore the fucking clickbait
SHOCKING!!!!   UNREAL!!!!
UNBELIEVABLE!!!!   INTENSE!!!!
HORRIFIC!!!!   HILARIOUS!!!!
UNTHINKABLE!!!!   WTF?!?!?!

Yes, your imagination is running wild and you're desperate to see what happened to the creepy man in the grainy CCTV footage or what that kid from your favourite childhood film looks like 30 years later. But you must be strong. You must resist. You might think that you're only wasting your own time, but every click has a cost, and your casual curiosity only encourages people to keep writing that crap.

∽

Put your phone on fucking silent

The days when people would spend hundreds of pounds a year on getting the latest 'Crazy Frog' ringtone for their phone are fortunately over. Fortunately for everyone, except maybe employees of Jamster Entertainment Group. Most people also seem to understand the concept that when *PING* you're on public transport *PING* it's really *PING*-ing annoying for the whole carriage *PING* to receive notifications from *PING* your WhatsApp group. The phone is right in fucking front of you, so you don't need any further notification than your eyes. Please, turn the fucking thing onto silent.

∽

The problem with the internet and social media is simply down to numbers. (Numbers, and maybe the whole data privacy thing that's starting to make us feel like we're living in a Philip K. Dick novel.) Not just the zeros and ones it's made up of, but number of friends, number of likes, number of posts, number of followers. Success is confirmed by how many times something was viewed and how many people commented. Algorithms and software are based on data and statistics, not human nature and gut instinct. Quantity is the winner on the internet, not quality.

It's up to each of us to moderate our own numbers, balance our online selves with our offline lives and set some fucking limits to what we post. Unless we start to put a little more consideration towards the endless twaddle that we thoughtlessly fart out into the internet, things will start to get seriously out of fucking control. Social media is barely a teenager and we're already seeing the dangers our digital footprint can cause us for jobs and interviews. Private lives are constantly broadcast in a public arena no matter what privacy settings we believe we've set. When was the last time you bothered to read a full Ts&Cs document for anything, rather than just lazily click 'allow'?

We need to set an example to the future generations, who will undoubtedly inhabit this online world more frequently, that we didn't abuse our freedom by acting like complete savages randomly shouting stuff at each other. We need to find some fucking balance instead of spamming our 'friends' with constant shite. You might not think Monica Lewinsky is the most credible source to quote, but having been dragged through one of the biggest witch-hunts of modern times, I'd argue she's better placed than most: 'We talk a lot about our right to freedom of expression, but we need to talk more about our responsibility to freedom of expression. We all want to be heard. But let's acknowledge the difference between speaking up with intention and speaking up for attention.'

With a bit of common sense, respect, restraint and compassion towards others when they fuck up, we can make the media we consume a little more social again.

~

TEN FUCKING
GOOD MANNERS

I've tried to cover as many areas as possible in this book, but I'm well aware there are some huge – and important – parts of life that I've missed out. But while some of you may be disappointed that you haven't learned the correct etiquette for exchanging wives at a local swingers party, or how long you should leave it before sending your first dickpic, I hope it's been useful in other ways.

What I did notice along the way though, was most fucking good manners seemed to fall into ten basic rules. Follow them as best you can – along with those other Ten Commandments – and you should be able to avoid any major fuck ups.

~

1) Leave things as
you fucking found them

Or, if possible, in a better state than when you found them. This applies to: train carriages, buses, planes (excl. Ryanair), cinema seats, public toilets, private toilets, gym equipment, changing rooms, cyclists, meeting rooms, saunas, phone boxes, parks, beaches, your sexy aunt's knicker drawer, workplace kitchens, supermarket trolleys, people's emotional state, holiday homes, pub tables, baby-changing units, hotel rooms, your neighbour's lawn, your home, your street, our planet.

~

2) Learn the difference between
private and public

What goes on in your home is your fucking business, but don't be surprised if people start getting shitty when you display similar manners in public. You may enjoy drying your genitals with a hairdryer at home, but don't do it in the swimming pool changing rooms. Adapt your behaviour to suit the world around you and we can hopefully all enjoy a bit of harmony. The same applies to social media – it's called the World Wide Web because it's world-fucking-wide. Whatever you may believe your privacy settings to be, once it's online, it's out there in the public.

~

3) Do one thing at a fucking time

People are busy. When people get busy they get fucking stressed. When people get fucking stressed they start behaving like the colic-suffering lovechild of Naomi Campbell and Justin Bieber. We've developed a whole plethora of devices to help us multitask, but the real trick is learning to fucking simplify what we do and enjoy our time doing it. Quality, not quantity.

Giving yourself more time means you've got more time to give to other people, and will greatly reduce the chance of you losing your shit when an old dear can't find her purse at the bus stop. As Philip Stanhope wrote in one of his letters to his son on 14 April 1747:

'There is time enough for everything, in the course of the day, if you do but one thing at once; but there is not time enough in the year, if you will do two things at a time.'

~

4) Take some fucking responsibility

We all have our slightly muddled reasons for our actions – a desperate justification or lame excuse for our spontaneous act of knobbishness. Sometimes the consequences of these are pretty fucking serious, and the temptation is to try to wriggle out of it, or pass the buck onto someone else. Whether it's in the workplace, the car, a posh yurt at a festival or the toilets in McDonald's, you need to face the fucking music. Dancing is optional.

∾

5) Be fucking grateful for what you've got

The chances are that if you're reading this book, you're not doing too fucking badly for yourself. No matter how stressful you might think things are, in the scheme of it all, you're doing OK. The majority of us are lucky enough to have homes and cars and food and access to online streaming services. But our desire to constantly fucking upgrade our lives and have more, means we're rarely satisfied with what we've got. Buy stuff, by all means, but look after it and take some fucking pride in making it last longer than you thought possible. As the old proverb goes: 'To live fully, we must learn to use things and love people, and not love things and use people.'

❧

6) Look after our planet

Treat it like it's the only fucking one we've got. Because it is. Buy less bottled water (or none at all if you can), get a reusable coffee cup, pick up some litter, buy less plastic, recycle more, share a car, eat less meat, eat more veg, turn off your lights, turn off your taps, fly less, look after your neighbourhood, resell your unwanted stuff, reuse your paper, scrape the mould off your jam, buy local, buy seasonal, get an allotment, stop washing with microbeads, print less, take the stairs, plant some trees and leave our planet in a reasonable state for the next generation. Thank you.

❧

7) Just fucking ignore them

Opinions, as we're often reminded, are like arseholes – everyone's got one, but no one thinks theirs stinks. Back in our tribal days when we lived in little communes of 150 people there was a much greater chance of people sharing the same views as us, but we're beyond that now. We need to accept that we're surrounded by millions of people with very fucking different opinions – and there are more than a few right twats out there. In fact, you're most likely one of those twats in the eyes of someone else. You don't have to like them or agree with them, but don't leap onto Twitter to call them out. As Republican presidential nominee Wendell Willkie said: 'The test of good manners is to be able to put up pleasantly with bad ones.'

～

8) Accept that life isn't fucking perfect

Not just in a material sense, but in an emotional one too. It's difficult in a world where we're constantly reminded of how 'good' life could be on social media: perfect abs, perfect teeth, perfect holidays, perfect car, perfect fucking manners, perfect diets, perfect trainers and TVs, perfect jobs, perfect immigration policies, perfect NHS, perfect equality. We spend so much time salivating over the end goal, that we forget to appreciate how far we've come. We judge life based on success and failure, rather than improvement, and in the process ignore the fucking great steps our society has made in the last 100 years. We may not have reached the top of the mountain, but we're heading in the right direction.

～

9) Put your fucking phone away

Phones are great, but don't let them take over your life. While *Chicago Tribune* columnist Mary Schmich (not Baz Luhrmann or Kurt Vonnegut) chose to praise the long-term benefits of sunscreen, if I could offer you one tip for the future, putting your fucking phone away would be it.

❧

10) When in doubt, choose kindness

Or, in other words, learn some fucking humility. Hold out an olive branch and show some genuine human compassion. It doesn't matter where you were born, where you went to school, how much you earn, what car you drive or what you were voted most likely to be at school, we should all be able to recognise when others require our help and prioritise that over our own sense of superiority. Take note of the example set by HM Queen Elizabeth II (or maybe it was Victoria, or maybe it's just an urban myth) who saw a guest take their finger dipping bowl, and, not knowing what it was for, start to drink from it. Rather than highlight his mistake in front of everyone, she spared his blushes by drinking from her own finger bowl, and other guests followed her example.

Whether it's true or not doesn't really matter. It's the perfect encapsulation of Dr Wayne W. Dyer's precept, adopted by R.J. Palacio in her novel *Wonder*: 'When given the choice between being right or being kind, choose kind.'[22]

CONCLUSION

❧

*'For civilization to survive, the human
race has to remain civilized.'*
ROD SERLING, *THE TWILIGHT ZONE*

❧

I've been well aware when writing this book that a large proportion of the people who will read it will probably have a decent grasp of the subject already. And perhaps the people who need it the most won't read past the first page. By simply showing an interest in manners you are already demonstrating a consideration towards others, and an appreciation that the world is not here purely for you to do whatever the fuck you want.

But the biggest question of all is: *Does it really fucking matter?* A study commissioned by *Sky Atlantic* in 2018 revealed that 71 per cent of people wished others would pay more attention to their manners and social etiquette. But the same survey showed 'a third are convinced there are greater benefits to being rude and breaking the rules of social etiquette.'[23]

Who cares if you leave your phone on in the cinema, eat steak three times a day or talk over the office temp who shouldn't have been in the fucking meeting in the first place. Manners are boring. Manners are difficult. Manners are for weak people. Being rude is funny. Being rude is quicker, easier and gets you what you fucking want.

It's difficult to argue with this, except that for society to keep working smoothly, you need cogs and you need oil. Without the oil the cogs will work for a bit, but sooner or later everything's going to go to shit. Likewise, too much oil and not enough cogs, and we don't get very far. Plus it's a potential fire hazard. The key is finding some balance, which is difficult because as well as having more cogs in the machine than at any other time, there are a large quantity of complete fucking spanners in there.

Fucking good manners are not about being conformist. We don't want to live in a world of head-nodding robots where everyone's overly nice to each other and scared to say anything for fear of causing offence. But we're not that fucking far off it – we're already recording each other's behaviour to get a few quid off the tabloids and rating every purchase we make – how long before we're the ones being rated (and not just our credit scores or online comments)?

We really don't want to go down that road, and I'd argue that the best way to avoid this kind of lunacy is to start to show some fucking good manners. We need to adopt the Queen's 'tried and tested recipes, like speaking well of each other and respecting different points of view'. We need to display our ability to be trusted and respectful before it's enforced on us.

The essence of manners hasn't really changed over the years, just the context that we apply them to. Whether it's Ptahhotep's wisdom to his son, Daniel of Beccles' advice on attacking enemies while they're defecating, or Giovanni Della Casa's tips on checking your bogeys, manners have always been about stepping out of your fucking bubble and looking at life from someone else's point of view.

This book is an attempt to try and highlight a few of the flash points where life can get a little tense, but it shouldn't be taken as a definitive list of Dos and Don'ts. It's up to each and every one of us to apply some common-fucking-sense to our own individual circumstances, create a set of standards to live by and make sure those standards aren't solely for the benefit of ourselves. The golden rule of 'Treat others as you'd like to be treated yourself' is great in principle, but increasingly difficult to enforce in a world where we can't even fucking agree whether a country should be in or out of the EU.

Like fucking apostrophes (the subject of my first book), fucking good manners are a lot more complicated than we tend to believe they are. Judging my own manners against what I've written over the last 40,000 words, I doubt I come out much better than a C+, or 'room for improvement' as school teachers would say. Of course I've had perfectly legitimate reasons for acting in this way – personal circumstances and situations that I've used to internally rationalise my crude behaviour – and we all do this. But just as we forgive ourselves for these minor or sometimes major lapses in judgement, we should be equally forgiving towards others.

There's no such thing as perfect manners in today's society. Just as our very existence on this planet means that we will have an impact on the environment, so we will inevitably have an impact on the people around us, and guess what? Not everyone's going to fucking like it. We can't stop that, but we can start to be tolerant and set an example for others to follow.

CONCLUSION

For all the ranty effing and jeffing in this book, the key is to take a deep breath and let it go. We all make mistakes – it's part of what makes us human, after all – but we can't spend our lives calling out other people's selfishness. We should only do our best to make sure that when our time on this planet comes to an end, we've done a little more of the fucking good stuff than the fucking bad stuff.

❧

ACKNOWLEDGEMENTS

This book hasn't been easy to write. In the back of my mind has always been my own dickish behaviour, so perhaps my first acknowledgement should be to anyone who has been at the receiving end of my own bad manners over the years. Sorry for whatever it was I did, and thank you for your tolerance.

Thanks also to everyone who was kind enough to send me books and general tips on manners: Amy, Clive, Siobhan, Lucy, Matt Colabraro, Em and Rich. Sorry if I haven't included them all. And to my parents for pointing me in the right direction for the last 42 years, no matter how far I drifted off course. To Jo, Matilda and Maurice, who, since I took on this project have taken great delight in pointing out my many bad manners, while displaying their own impeccable standards. And to Di and Colin for the sanctuary of your flat in Scarborough while I was writing this.

Thanks again to Dave, Sue, Adam, Ollie, Amy, Mike, Jon and Tim at Music in Manchester (music. agency) who took a chance back in 2015 and helped me achieve something I never thought possible. And to David Marsh at *The Guardian* who turned a little book on apostrophes into something far bigger than I ever imagined.

A special thanks to all those at Icon Books who have encouraged me to put fingertip to keyboard once again, and for your ongoing support over the last year. Philip for your pep-talk among general chat about cricket, Duncan and Andrew for giving me the opportunity in the first place, and Ellen for your professionalism, diligence and eternal patience when I emailed late on a Friday saying it wouldn't be ready for another week.

And finally thanks to Rocky Flintstone, Belinda Missen, Jo, Robin, J.P. Willson, Georgina, Tracey Allen, Joe, Bill, John Naylor, Carolyn Halliday, April Helems, Wattanit Hotrakool, Meaghan Steeves, Jackie, Kate, Gina, Kest Schwartzman, Ems, Crimes, Lora Davis, Rachel, Mimi, Anis Zainudin, Ellen, Alysha, Miss G, Anna Shahbazyan, Merce, Usagi Alice, Vanessa, Gayle Arrey, Kristine, Lizzy Pollard, Andrea, Jess Evans, Stephanie Spafford, Bart King, Eileen Bright, Kelly, Anyuita,

ACKNOWLEDGEMENTS

Noone Tsang, Ulrike, Emma Haddock, Diego Alexandro, Melissa Carlson, Angharad Lodwick, Abdelhakamziyad Kuma, Jade du Preez, Jenny Broach, Jatin Lalwani, John Bradley, Ruthy Baker, Selin, Molly Rookwood, Sue, Jake Graham, Peter Gerrie, Jennifer, Tim Hart, Paige Bolland, Gertrude and Lola, Mallory, Malini Nair, Checri, Ashleigh Lister, Karen Payton, Rupi Singh, Amy Stettler, Kate, Kate, Jocelyn, Ann, Ann Day, Fay Kinnitt, Stephanie, Mugren Ohaly and Amanda Carlyle for your five-star reviews of my last book on Goodreads. It means a lot, and I hope you've enjoyed this one too.

∾

NOTES

1. 'Robin Dunbar: we can only ever have 150 friends at most . . .', *The Guardian*, 14 March 2010: https://www.theguardian.com/technology/2010/mar/14/my-bright-idea-robin-dunbar

2. Emily Post Quotations: https://emilypost.com/aboutemily-postquotations/

3. Daniel of Beccles, *Urbanus Magnus – The Book of the Civilised Man*, A. Deed Frith: 2007

4. Giovanni Della Casa, *Galateo: Or, the Rules of Polite Behavior*, University of Chicago Press: 2013

5. Philip Dormer Stanhope Chesterfield, *Letters to His Son on the Art of Becoming a Man of the World and a Gentleman, 1746–47*, Amazon Kindle Unlimited

6. Emily Post, *Etiquette in Society, In Business, In Politics, and at Home*, Open Road Media: 2017

7. Reproduced from *The Better Angels of Our Nature* by Steven Pinker, published by Penguin Books. With permission from Penguin Books Ltd. Copyright © Steven Pinker, 2011

8. Alexandra Ma, 'China has started ranking citizens with a creepy 'social credit' system – here's what you can do wrong, and the embarrassing, demeaning ways they can punish you' *Business Insider*, 29 October 2018: https://www.businessinsider.com/china-social-credit

-system-punishments-and-rewards-explained-2018
-4?r=US&IR=T

9. Robert A. Heinlein, *Time Enough for Love*, Ace; Reissue edition: 1987

10. 'Road rage: This is how many people have fallen victim in the last year', *Daily Express*, 31 May 2017: https://www.express.co.uk/life-style/cars/811471/Road-rage-UK-driving-motorist-car-research

11. Clive Hamilton, *Growth Fetish*, Australia: Allen & Unwin, 2003. Reprinted with permission of the publisher.

12. George Monbiot, 'Consumer Hell', *The Guardian*, 5 January 2010: https://www.monbiot.com/2010/01/04/consumer-hell/

13. 'Chaos at Black Friday sale in Vancouver, shirtless man uses belt as a whip', CTVnews, 27 November 2016: https://www.ctvnews.ca/canada/chaos-at-black-friday-sale-in-vancouver-shirtless-man-uses-belt-as-a-whip-1.3178977

   'Huge Black Friday riot breaks out over discounted TOILET ROLLS in South African supermarket', *Mirror*, 25 November 2016: https://www.mirror.co.uk/news/world-news/huge-black-friday-fight-breaks-9331697

   '"They are like animals": Nutella sale sparks Black Friday-style riots at supermarkets throughout France', *Evening Standard*, 26 January 2018: https://www.standard.co.uk/news/world/they-are-like-animals-nutella-sale-sparks-blac-fridaystyle-chaos-at-supermarkets-across-france-a3750056.html

   'Angry shoppers square off in pre-Black Friday scuffle at Palmdale Walmart, authorities say', *LA Times*, 23 November 2018: https://www.latimes.com/local/

lanow/la-me-ln-black-friday-fight-palmdale-20181123-story.html

14. '"Pls entertain me": shortage of Black Friday brawls prompts online gripes', *The Guardian*, 23 November 2018: https://www.theguardian.com/business/2018/nov/23/black-friday-fights-viral-video-backlash

15. From *The Undertaking: Life Studies From the Dismal Trade by Thomas Lynch*. Published in the UK by Vintage. Reprinted by permission of The Random House Group Limited. © 1998. USA: Copyright © 1997 by Thomas Lynch. Used by permission of W. W. Norton & Company, Inc.

16. 'If', Rudyard Kipling, 1943

17. 'TripAdvisor reveals world's 10 worst tourist attractions for queues', News.com.au, 18 August 2017: https://www.news.com.au/travel/world-travel/europe/tripadvisor-reveals-worlds-10-worst-tourist-attractions-for-queues/news-story/8c08159e8366cb2fcfa83aeaedbafce3

18. 'Viral email humiliations: from resignation letters to "hottest in the office" lists', *Telegraph*, 30 March 2011: https://www.telegraph.co.uk/news/newstopics/howaboutthat/8414829/Viral-email-humiliations-from-resignation-letters-to-hottest-in-the-office-lists.html

19. 'The 6 Most Disastrous Uses of Work Email Ever', *Cracked*, 4 October 2008: https://www.cracked.com/article_16690_the-6-most-disastrous-uses-work-email-ever.html

20. Monica Lewinsky: 'The Price of Shame', TED, 20 March 2015: https://www.youtube.com/watch?v=H_8y0WLm78U

21. '9 Of The Funniest Twitter Hashtag Hash-Ups', *Sabotage Times*, 14 April 2015: https://sabotagetimes.com/

life/now-that-cher-is-dead-and-8-other-hilarious-hashtag-hash-ups

22. From *Wonder* by R.J. Palacio. Published by Corgi. Reprinted by permission of The Random House Group Limited © 2014

23. 'The Old-Fashioned Manners in Danger of Dying Out', *Independent*, 27 January 2018: https://www.independent.co.uk/life-style/manners-danger-dying-out-a8164571.html

BIBLIOGRAPHY

Amy Alkon, *Good Manners For Nice People Who Sometimes Say F*ck*, St Martin's Griffin: 2014

Bodleian Lib, *The Art of Good Manners*, The Bodleian Library: 2014

Mark Caldwell, *A Short History of Rudeness: Manners, Morals, and Misbehavior in Modern America*, Picador USA: 2000

Gerald Carson, *The Polite Americans: A Wide-Angle View of Our More or Less Good Manners Over 300 Years*, Praeger Publishers Inc: 1980

Charles William Day, *Hints on Etiquette and the Usages of Society (1834)*, printed for Longman, Orme, Brown, Green & Longmans; 2nd edition: 1836

Debrett's A-Z of Modern Manners, Debrett's Ltd: 2018

Meghan Doherty, *How Not To Be A Dick*, Zest Books: 2013

Norbert Y. Elias, *The History of Manners: 1 (The Civilizing Process)*, Random House USA Inc: 1988

P.M. Forni, *Choosing Civility: The Twenty-Five Rules of Considerate Conduct*, St. Martin's Griffin: 2002

Malcolm Gladwell, *The Tipping Point*, Abacus: 2002

Henry Hitchings, *Sorry! The English and their Manners*, John Murray: 2014

Steven Pinker, *The Better Angels of Our Nature*, Penguin: 2012

Jon Ronson, *So You've Been Publicly Shamed*, Picador: 2015

∽

ABOUT THE AUTHOR

Simon Griffin has worked as a copywriter in advertising and design for over twenty years. In that time he's learnt the importance of listing big clients that you've worked for, such as Procter & Gamble, Nike, Sony, Microsoft and Savills, without saying exactly what you did for them, or even whether the work was any good. His writing has been recognised by D&AD, Design Week, Cannes, *Creative Review*, New York Festivals and Epica, and he's also been on the Writing for Design Jury at D&AD. In 2016 his first book *Fucking Apostrophes* became an international bestseller, featuring in *The Guardian*, on BBC Radio 5Live, Australia's ABC News and *The Wall Street Journal*. While researching and writing *Fucking Good Manners* he decided to politely wave goodbye to the world of advertising and design, and is currently retraining to be a school teacher. Fortunately for children and parents across the Yorkshire region, he doesn't really swear that much.

ALSO AVAILABLE

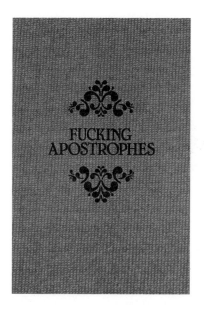

The title says it all. Despite what some
might claim, the rules about how to use
apostrophes are complicated, and have
evolved haphazardly. This is a light-hearted
guide to getting the fucking things right.

'At last, a book that tells you exactly where to
stick your apostrophe . . . funny and useful,
the perfect stocking filler.' David Marsh, *Guardian*

ISBN: 9781785781414 (hardback)
ISBN: 9781785781421 (ebook)